Development Education

Development Education
Debates and dialogue

Edited by Douglas Bourn

First published in 2008 by the Institute of Education, University of London,
20 Bedford Way, London WC1H 0AL
www.ioe.ac.uk/publications

British Library Cataloguing in Publication Data:
A catalogue record for this publication is available from the British Library

ISBN 978 0 85473 803 8

Page make up by Hobbs the Printers Ltd, Totton, Hampshire SO40 3WX
Printed by Elanders www.elanders.com

Contents

Contributors

Vanessa Andreotti is a senior lecturer at the School of Maori, Social and Cultural Studies in Education at the University of Canterbury, New Zealand. She is also a Research Fellow at the Development Education Research Network at the National University of Ireland in Galway, and the Centre for the Study of Social and Global Justice at the University of Nottingham. Her research interests include postcolonial theory and global citizenship education.

Barbara Asbrand is Professor of Education at Göttingen University and was previously research fellow at the University of Erlangen-Nürnberg, Germany. Her research is focused on global learning, quality education and evaluation and educational anthropology.

Douglas Bourn is Director of the Development Education Research Centre, Institute of Education, University of London. He was previously Director of the Development Education Research Centre (DEA). He is Chair of the UNESCO UK Committee on Education for Sustainable Development.

David Hicks is Professor in the School of Education, Bath Spa University and author of a number of publications on global and futures education.

Anna Luise Laycock is Learning Co-ordinator for Oxfam Education and Youth. She holds an MSc in Global Ethics, specialising in global citizenship, and has worked in the education and fair trade sectors.

Alison Leonard is a research student at the Development Education Research Centre, Institute of Education, geography teacher at Westminster School, London, and lecturer at Canterbury Christ Church University for the Teach First programme.

Annette Scheunpflug is Professor of Education at the University of Erlangen-Nürnberg, Germany. Her research is focused on global learning, international and intercultural education, educational anthropology and quality in education. She is a member of the advisory board for development education of the German Ministry of Economic Cooperation and Development.

Gillian Temple is Head of Oxfam's Education and Youth Team. She has extensive experience as a teacher and school inspector, and has worked with numerous charities, local education authorities and government departments.

Preface

This publication is the first to emerge from the Development Education Research Centre of the Institute of Education, University of London. The Centre was established in 2006 with financial support from the Department for International Development (DFID) with the aim of raising the profile and support for development education within higher education. The primary functions of the Centre are to promote debate and dialogue on development education within higher education, to develop an international network of interested academics and researchers, and to identify and undertake research that relates to the needs and agendas of the sector.

The chapters in this volume are based on, or closely linked to, papers presented at the Development Education: Policy, practice and theory conference held at the Institute in November 2006 and organised in partnership with the Development Education Association. They reflect a range of opinions and perspectives on development education and related themes of global education, global learning and global citizenship, not only from the UK, but also Germany and Brazil. They will stimulate debate and dialogue, identify issues and themes for research, and pose questions that development education practitioners need to consider.

Development education and its related terms have been around since the 1970s but they have had a difficult history. As the issues that development education has raised are now becoming more central within debates in education, the contribution it has made and can continue to make will hopefully receive greater recognition and support.

I would like to thank my colleagues at the Institute of Education for their support, advice and comments on the following chapters.

Douglas Bourn

1 Introduction

Douglas Bourn

A range of terms has been used to describe learning and understanding about the wider world including 'development education', 'global education', 'global learning' and 'global citizenship'. This introductory chapter aims to provide a historical context for these terms and how they have been interpreted and then summarise how the other authors in this volume have related their own conceptual framework to the need for further debate, dialogue and research.

Historical context

The term development education first emerged during the 1970s, in part in response to the growth of development and aid organisations and the decolonisation process, but also, as Harrison (2005) has commented, through the influence of UNESCO and the United Nations which in 1975 defined it as follows:

> Development education is concerned with issues of human rights, dignity, self-reliance, and social justice in both developed and developing countries. It is concerned with the causes of underdevelopment and the promotion of an understanding of what is involved in development, of how different countries go about undertaking development, and of the reasons for and ways of achieving a new international economic and social order.
>
> (United Nations 1975, quoted in Osler 1994)

By the end of the 1970s, however, the term was increasingly being used in a narrower sense, as governments and non-governmental organisations (NGOs) engaged in the development sector sought public support and involvement. In the UK, the Labour government of that period created an advisory committee on development education; the emphasis of their interest and funding was to support 'those processes of thought and action which increase understanding of worldwide social, economic, and political conditions, particularly those which relate to, and are responsible for, under-development' (ODA 1978).

During the 1980s, two broader influences began to have an impact on development education. The first was the thinking of Paulo Freire (1972) and the writings of Julius Nyerere, with their views on the relationship of education to social change. Alongside this was the influence of what Harrison (2005) calls the 'globalist' approach through the World Studies Project led by Robin Richardson and later Simon Fisher and Dave Hicks, and the work of David Selby and Graham Pike. This approach that emphasises an approach to learning about the world, rather than specifically about poverty, came to have considerable influence during this period (Fisher and Hicks 1985; Hicks 1990; Hicks 2003; Pike and Selby 1998; Richardson 1976).

Throughout the 1980s in the UK, and mirrored in other industrialised countries, development education was perceived as being closely allied to social democratic politics and an overtly political agenda. Funding therefore became related to the political outlook of the government. In the UK, development education, world studies and global education agendas came under political attack (McCollum 1996; Marshall 2005a). Similar debates were also taking place in North America (Cronkhite 2000) and it was only in countries such as the Netherlands and Sweden and in the European Commission that political support for development education grew during this period (Osler 1994).

It was therefore left to NGOs to play the leading role in promoting and delivering development education, particularly within schools (Arnold 1987, Sinclair, in Osler 1994). Key to the future, Sinclair suggested, was the need for NGOs to work in partnership with teachers, to be more strategic and to engage in academic debate.

By the late 1980s in the UK, as in other European countries, networks of NGOs were emerging to share and coordinate practice on development education. This resulted in an emerging consensus on the most appropriate terminology to use.

Definitions of development education

In the UK the definition of development education that became the framework for this practice was the one initiated by the National Association of Development Education Centres (NADEC), which in 1993 became subsumed within the newly created umbrella body, the Development Education Association (DEA):

Development education is about:

- enabling people to understand the links between their own lives and those of people throughout the world;
- increasing understanding of the global economic, social and political environmental forces which shape our lives;
- developing the skills, attitudes and values which enable people to work together to bring about change and to take control of their own lives;
- working to achieve a more just and sustainable world in which power and resources are equitably shared.

(DEA 2006)

This definition remains as the underlying framework for NGOs not only in the UK but across Europe. However, in both the DEA and the European Development Education Network, the following descriptions are used to summarise their members' practice:

Development education is an active learning process, founded on values of solidarity, equality, inclusion and co-operation. It enables people to move from basic awareness of international development

priorities and sustainable human development, through
understanding of the causes and effects of global issues, to personal
involvement and informed action.
(Development Education Exchange in Europe Project (DEEEP) 2007)

Development education is an approach to learning that leads to a
greater understanding of (global) inequalities, of why they exist and
what can be done about them. It encourages learners of all ages to
explore how global issues, such as poverty, link in with their everyday
lives. By challenging stereotypes and encouraging independent
thinking, development education aims to help people develop the
practical skills and confidence to make positive changes locally and
globally.
(DEA, no date)

A feature of both these definitions is the emphasis on a process of learning that is about understanding global inequality and promotion of action for change.

Whilst there may be a consensus amongst NGOs as to what constitutes the key themes of development education, the terminology used to articulate it or even promote it rarely uses the term 'development'. Terms such as 'global dimension', 'global citizenship' 'global education' or, in the context of specific areas of education, 'global youth work', 'global perspectives in higher education' and, within adult education, 'global learning' are all common. These terms have been used because they are perceived as being accessible and easier to understand within educational practice (Bourn 2003).

In this volume, a range of terms is used, including global education, global learning and education for global citizenship. In part they reflect the complex roots of development education, but they also reflect the lack of clarity as to its specific focus and contribution to broader educational debates. Even the membership of the DEA, in a survey conducted in April 2007, in answer to a question as to which terms best communicate what they do, in order of preference responded: Global Education, Global Citizenship and Education for Global Justice/Citizenship (DEA 2007).

4

Policy debates

The Department for International Development (DFID), the ministry in the UK that has given considerable resources to funding development education since 1997, has stated that its primary objective is to go beyond 'attitudes to development based on compassion and charity,' and to establish 'a real understanding of our interdependence and the relevance of development issues to people's everyday lives' (DFID 1998).

In Ireland, NGOs and policy-makers have also emphasised the relationship between development education and the broader development agenda.

> These difficult questions (of inequality and injustice internationally) lie at the heart of the work that is now needed ... education for world democracy, for human rights and for sustainable human development is no longer an option. Education has a central role to play, especially if we are to build a widespread understanding and ownership of this (development) agenda.
>
> (Development Education Ireland 2007)[1]

These approaches however could be perceived as being at odds with that of the European Union (EU), a key funder of NGOs. Key to EU funding criteria for support 'is the mobilisation of public action and support in Europe for development'.[2]

McCollum (1996) and Marshall (2005a) have also suggested that the lack of clarity about development education is linked not only to the conflicting pressures of government funding, but also the needs of the education system and relationships with the South and the developing world.

The needs of the UK and other Northern-based education systems are being increasingly influenced by the impact of globalisation and the needs of a highly skilled economy. Tony Blair, for example, stated, 'Our young people must develop the competence, confidence and contacts which will secure their place and influence in an increasingly globalised society' (Central Bureau 1999).

UK government policy statements, whether on the narrower skills focus such as in the Leitch Review or the international education strategy, 'Putting the World into World Class Education' (DfES 2004), pose the debates in the context of people playing an active role in the global market. The Department for Education and Skills (DfES) strategy up to 2006 states that 'we can only create wealth through the knowledge, skills and enterprise of our people. We must measure our education and training performance against international benchmarks, learning from the best of international experience and sharing good practice' (DfES 2004).

The need for education to respond to the challenges of the global labour market were reinforced in the UK government's White Paper on the future of higher education: 'In a fast changing and increasingly competitive world, the role of higher education in equipping the labour force with appropriate and relevant skills, in stimulating innovation and supporting productivity and in enriching the quality of life, is central' (DfES 1999). Such economy-based policy responses obscure the wider issues posed by the challenge of globalisation for education. For the question which must be asked is whether the purpose of education is to equip people to work within the global economy, or to provide the knowledge, skills and values base to understand and interpret the changing world so that people can be more active and engaged citizens.

It would be difficult to argue against education being seen as essential to a competitive knowledge-based global economy. Yet, as Alexander (1998) has stated, even embracing this dominant view can pose major questions:

- How does the global economy work, and what can people do to influence it?
- What is and should be the relationship between global, regional, national and local economies?
- How does the global economy affect the environment and sustainable development?
- How does decision-making affect citizenship?

Whether or not such questions are addressed depends to some extent upon the educational approach adopted. Education in the early twenty-first century is inevitably linked to globalisation, but what form of education are we talking about?

Green (1997) has suggested that the scope for education to act as a socially integrative force in contemporary society is not necessarily diminished or impeded by the forces of globalisation and post modernity. He further suggests that the West has perhaps shown little support for the goals of social cohesion and solidarity.

It could be argued that since 1997, in the UK at least, these goals are back on the agenda, in response in part to national and international events, and manifested in the introduction of citizenship education and the recognition of the importance of values within the school curriculum. But there is as yet little evidence or research, apart from the summary of the work undertaken by Asbrand in Germany (outlined in Chapter 3 in this volume), that begins to address where and how development education and global learning relate to globalisation.

Another theme suggested by McCollum (1996) and Marshall (2005a) that needs to be addressed is the relationship between the North and the South and its connections to debates regarding universalism versus multiple perspectives. As government policy-makers and funders increasingly promote the value of international partnerships, based on liberal notions of friendship and mutual learning (Harrison 2005; Leonard, Chapter 5 in this volume), it is necessary, as McCloskey has stated, to be 'receptive to and learn from the experiences and practices of the developing world' (McCann and McCloskey 2003).

Caserta, the coordinator of the European Development Education Network, suggests that partnerships between the North and the South are key to development education. He further proposes that it is through this model that the link to the global processes of development and eradication of poverty can ensure that development education is built on values of solidarity, inclusion and cooperation (Caserta 2005).

Academic debates on development education

The term development education is not well known within academic research and debate. When there has been academic discussion on the role and nature of development education, it was either during the 1970s and 1980s when it was linked to perceptions and roles of government and NGOs (Lemaresquier 1987; Brodhead 1986; McCollum 1996) or more recently in relation to debates on global citizenship (Marshall 2005a; Davies *et al.* 2005; Osler and Vincent 2002; Ibrahim 2005).

Audrey Osler's edited collection of essays *Development Education* (1994) provides an overview of development education across Europe. It is the only major publication in the past fifteen years that has specifically addressed the subject, although publications by Hicks and Holden (2007), Osler and Vincent (2002) and Steiner (1996) draw on development education perspectives and practices.

As support for development education began to increase, a number of research studies emerged that reflected on why progress and support for this area had been so difficult. McCollum (1996) suggests that a key issue was the culture of the practice of many people engaged in development education. Blum (2000) suggests that the roles and agendas of many NGOs were also problematic in terms of seeking predetermined conclusions. In the UK, with the election of a Labour government, several studies addressed the extent to which the independence and radical nature of much of earlier NGO practice was becoming compromised by government funding (Cameron and Fairbrass 2004; Hammond 2002).

Themes in this volume

The chapters in this volume, whilst recognising progress in the support and nature of practice since the 1990s, aim to address the relevance and contribution of development education and its related terms of global education, global learning and global citizenship to wider

8

educational debates. They further pose the need for research and evidence to be gathered to assess the contribution of development education to learning within a global society of the twenty-first century. Above all they aim to demonstrate that the issues raised by development education practice are key educational questions for today.

Some chapters are based on empirical research whilst others reflect ongoing debates within NGOs.

In Chapter 2, Annette Scheunpflug, Professor of Education at the University of Erlangen-Nürnberg, Germany, outlines why global education/learning is important for people living in a globalised world. Taking the ideas of Immanuel Kant on global social justice as a universal obligation and the importance of education in order to become an autonomous world citizen, Scheunpflug poses the implications of these perspectives for the theory and practice of global education/learning. In particular, she addresses: the need to make a distinction between learning and support for predetermined campaigns; and the view that the issues global education/learning pose are by their very nature controversial.

Gillian Temple and Anna Luise Laycock from Oxfam's Education and Youth Team in the UK take a different perspective in Chapter 6, using their 'education for global citizenship framework' to demonstrate the relationship between learning and action for change. They suggest there is a need to be more explicit in the agenda with young people, as a values-driven vision for change. They further suggest that active global citizenship means little unless it has a destination of a better world.

Barbara Asbrand, Professor of Education in Göttingen, Germany, outlines in Chapter 3 the main research findings of a qualitative research project on young people's knowledge about the world and their ability to act in a world society. Two main reasons are addressed: how young people respond and deal with living in a complex society, and the role that gender plays in dealing with uncertainty. She takes a different position from Temple and Laycock in that global education and global learning are not about teaching specific values but about enabling young people to find their own opinions.

In Chapter 4, Vanessa Andreotti, a Brazilian educator, uses a post-colonial framework to examine notions of development and poverty in relation to a critique of the 2000 edition of the UK government's 'Developing a Global Dimension in the School Curriculum' guidance document. Through a detailed contextual analysis of the publication, she addresses how terms like poverty are posed in relation to helplessness, and development in relation to economic and social progress. In comparison with Temple and Laycock, Andreotti questions the notion of a universal epistemology based around the goal of global citizenship education as an ideal.

Alison Leonard, a UK researcher on development education, in Chapter 5 uses the example of school linking to pose the need for critical reflection on the underlying power relationship between the North and the South in these partnership programmes. In reviewing the current debates and literature on the subject, Leonard identifies the need for major research in this area, particularly in the light of the UK government giving it a high priority, although there is little evidence yet as to its long-term value and impact.

David Hicks, Professor of Education in the UK, whilst welcoming the growth of interest in development education and the UK government's Global Dimension curriculum publication, suggests that a missing dimension is the notion of futures education. He outlines what he sees as the key concepts for this dimension and how it could contribute to the debates on images and perceptions young people have about the world. He poses the need for more research in these areas.

The chapters therefore identify, from a range of different perspectives, approaches and priorities, the following key issues:

- location of development education in relation to support for development and the needs of education systems in Northern countries;

- influence of universalist principles, multiple perspectives and postcolonial critiques of Western discourses;

- learning and action for social change;
- notions and perceptions of development, poverty and North–South relationships;
- role of gendered perspectives in understanding and support for development issues;
- inclusion of broader dimensions and concepts within development education debates, including a futures dimension.

Behind the lack of clarity within debates on the purpose of development education is the influence of conflicting policy drivers, particularly funding agendas.

Global citizenship

A major influence within NGO practice in the UK, and increasingly within schools, is Oxfam's framework of education for global citizenship, explored in relation to action for change by Temple and Laycock in Chapter 6. This framework brings together some of the debates around power relations, and promotes concepts of universal principles, linking them to action for change. For Oxfam (2006), the global citizen:

- is aware of the wider world and has a sense of their own role as a world citizen;
- respects and values diversity;
- has an understanding of how the world works economically, politically, socially, culturally, technologically and environmentally;
- challenges social injustice;

- participates in and contributes to the community at a range of levels from the local to the global;

- is willing to act to make the world a more equitable and sustainable place;

- takes responsibility for their own actions.

Questions as to what is 'global citizenship' have also been posed by Dower and Williams (2002) in relation to global social responsibility and the role of international structures. Key to the debate on global citizenship is the issue of universal values versus multiple perspectives, as outlined in this volume from different standpoints by Temple and Laycock (Chapter 6) and Andreotti (Chapter 4). Walker (2006) has posed this in relation to the 'apparent tension between diversity and our common humanity, the importance of intercultural understanding and the search for a set of universal values to unite humankind'.

Learning, action and social change

Finally, it is suggested that, in addition to issues regarding development and educational agendas, North–South relations and universal versus multiple perspectives, there is the need to address the constant underlying theme within development education practice of learning linked to action for change. The varying definitions of development education outlined at the beginning of this chapter suggest that from raising awareness to a process of learning, social action will somehow emerge because people will have gained a degree of consciousness based on a sense of emotional outrage at the levels of global social injustice and inequality. From a number of perspectives, this definition is challenged because it does not take sufficient account of the complex nature of how people learn and the relationships between learning, experience and personal action.

Development education practice by its very nature implies

approaches towards learning that challenge dominant ideological frameworks regarding the purpose, nature and form of education (Apple 2001; Marshall 2005b). A criticism often made of development education in the past (Arnold 1987; Smillie 1994) has been that it did not constantly seek to reflect upon its relationship to the dominant educational discourses of the time. As McCollum (1996) has stated, 'development education has been a movement which speaks only to itself, it has not located itself within a broader critical pedagogical discourse'. Today, as development education practice appears to be listened to more than ever by policy-makers, the relationship to learning and social change becomes even more critical.

Key to moving the debate forward therefore is a recognition, as Jarvis suggests, of the relationship between learning and personal interaction: human learning only occurs when individuals are consciously aware of a situation and respond, or try to respond, meaningfully to what they experience; and then seek to reproduce or transform and integrate the outcome into their own biographies (Jarvis *et al.* 2003).

If learning also implies change, as the Campaign for Learning stated – 'a process of active engagement with experience' and what people do 'to make sense of the world' (quoted in Dillon 2003) – then development education needs to look much more at questions of identity, personal involvement and motivations for action. As Dillon (2003) suggests, learning is not about transmission of knowledge and skills in a passive manner; rather we build (construct) knowledge through social interaction. Beck (2000) states that in addressing the needs of a rapidly changing society, learning must be about seeking to understand and to be critically aware of the things being studied.

Stimulus for debate and dialogue

As the following chapters demonstrate, there is a need for more debate on where and how development education locates itself in relation both to policy changes on education and development and to theoretical questions regarding learning and social change.

It is not intended here to pose any conclusions as to what development education should be in the future, but rather, at a time of rapid economic and social change, to invite reflection on the relevance of development education's themes and perspectives to education today.

It is hoped that these contributions by a range of academics, researchers and practitioners will stimulate more research, debate and dialogue on an area of education that has potentially much to offer, but is still perceived as being in the margins of academic discourse.

Development education needs above all to be located in an approach to learning which is about reflection, sharing and testing new ideas, providing conceptual inputs and learning from practice and experience. It needs to move away from being a list of noble intentions or even a series of bodies of knowledge, skills and values towards being an approach to learning. This means that debates and discussions should be contested; there should be critical dialogue and debate and space for a range of voices, views and perspectives.

Conclusions

Development education and its related terms of global learning, global education and global citizenship emerged initially as a response to political and NGO calls for learning and understanding about the wider world. As the practice has evolved, issues have continued to emerge about the relationship between learning, action and social change. This is a theme that is developed further in this volume. Similarly, what and how young people learn about global and development issues and the relationship of this learning to broader social and cultural influences are also considered. Finally, how development education relates to broader questions of learning, in particular in challenging dominant educational orthodoxy, is addressed. If development education is to have an impact on the academic and research community it needs to begin to grapple with these wider questions. This volume offers a contribution to this debate.

Notes

1 These ideas are developed further through a very informative website: <www.developmenteducationireland.ie>

2 For background to European Commission funding see: <www.ec.europa.eu/europeaid/projects/ ong_cd/ed_page_en.htm>

References

Alexander, T. (1998) 'Are we ready for the Age of Global Learning?' *Development Education Journal*, 5.1, 32.

Apple, M. (2001) *Educating the 'Right Way': Markets, standards, God and inequality.* London: Routledge/Falmer.

Arnold, S. (1987) *Constrained Crusaders: NGOs and development education in the UK.* Occasional Paper, Institute of Education, University of London.

Beck, U. (2000) *What Is Globalisation?* Cambridge: Polity Press.

Blum, N. (2000) 'Doing development at home: education as a tool for social change'. MA dissertation, University of Sussex.

Bourn, D. (2003) 'Towards a theory of development education'. *Development Education Journal*, 10.1, 3–6.

Brodhead, T. (1986) 'Development education and Northern governments'. In *Development Education: The state of the art.* Geneva: NGLS.

Caserta, A. (2005) 'Development exchange in Europe'. *Policy and Practice*, 1, 38–45.

Cameron, J. and Fairbrass, S. (2004) 'From development awareness to enabling effective support: the changing profile of development education in England'. *Journal of International Development*, 16, 729–40.

Central Bureau (1999) *Annual Report.* London: Central Bureau/British Council.

Cronkhite, L. (2000) 'Development education: making connections North and South' In D. Selby and T. Goldstein (eds), *Weaving Connections.* Toronto: Sumach Press.

Davies, I., Evans, M. and Reid, A. (2005) 'Globalising citizenship education? A critique of global education and citizenship education'. *British Journal of Educational Studies*, 55.1, 66–89.

Department for Education and Skills (DfES) (1999) *The Learning Age*, London: HMSO.

—— (2004) *Putting the World into World Class Education*. London: HMSO.

—— (2005) *Developing a Global Dimension in the School Curriculum*, revised edition. London: DfES.

Department for International Development (DFID) (1998) *Eliminating World Poverty: A challenge for the 21st century*. London: HMSO.

Development Education Association (DEA) (no date) *Development Education Association: Promoting change through education*. London: DEA.

—— (2006) Annual Report. London: DEA.

—— (2007) Report of views on priorities of future work of DEA. Online. Available HTTP: <http://www.dea.org.uk/consultations> (accessed 1 July 2007).

Development Education Exchange in Europe Project (DEEEP) (2007) Definitions of development education. Online. Available HTTP: <http://www.deeep.org./whatisde/definitions> (accessed 30 June 2007).

Development Education Ireland (2007) Definitions of development education. Online. Available HTTP: <http://www.developmenteducationireland.ie>

Dillon, J. (2003) 'On learners and learning in environmental education: missing theories, ignored communities'. *Environmental Education Research*, 2.3, 215–26.

Dower, N. and Williams, J. (eds) (2002) *Global Citizenship: A critical introduction*. New York: Routledge.

Fisher, S. and Hicks, D. (1985) *World Studies 8–13*. Edinburgh: Oliver & Boyd.

Freire, P. (1972) *Pedagogy of the Oppressed*. Harmondsworth: Penguin.

Green, A. (1997) *Education, Globalisation and the Nation State*. Basingstoke: Macmillan.

Hammond, B (2002) 'DFID's invisible hand: a challenge to development education?' Unpublished MA dissertation, University of East Anglia.

Harrison, D. (2005) 'Post-Its on history of development education'. *Development Education Journal*, 13.1, 6–8.

Hicks, D. (1990) 'World studies 8–13: a short history, 1980–89'. *Westminster Studies in Education*, 13, 61–80.

—— (2003) 'Thirty years of global education'. *Education Review*, 265–75.

Hicks, D. and Holden, C. (eds) (2007) *Teaching the Global Dimension*. London: Routledge.

Ibrahim, T. (2005) 'Global citizenship education: mainstreaming the curriculum?' *Cambridge Journal of Education*, 35.2, 177–94.

Jarvis, P, Holford, J. and Griffin, C. (2003) *The Theory and Practice of Learning*. London: Kogan Page.

Lemaresquier, T. (1987) 'Prospects for development education: some strategic issues facing European NGOs'. *World Development*, 15, Supplement, 189–200.

Marshall, H. (2005a) 'The sociology of global education: power, pedagogy and practice'. Unpublished PhD thesis, University of Cambridge.

—— (2005b) 'Developing the global gaze in citizenship education: exploring the perspectives of global education NGO workers in England'. *International Journal of Citizenship and Teacher Education*, 1.2, 76–92.

McCann, G. and McCloskey, S. (eds) (2003) *From the Local to the Global*. London: Pluto.

McCollum, A. (1996) 'On the margins? An analysis of theory and practice of development education in the1990s'. Unpublished PhD thesis, Open University.

Osler, A. (ed.) (1994) *Development Education*. London: Cassells.

Osler, A. and Vincent, K. (2002) *Citizenship and the Challenge of Global Education*. Stoke-on-Trent: Trentham.

Overseas Development Administration (ODA) (1978) *Development Education: Report of Advisory Committee*. London: HMSO.

Oxfam (2006) *Education for Global Citizenship*. Oxford: Oxfam.

Pike, G. and Selby, D. (1998) *Global Teacher, Global Learner*. Sevenoaks: Hodder & Stoughton.

Richardson, R. (1976) *Learning for Change in World Society*. London: World Studies Project.

Smillie, I. (1994) 'Changing partners: Northern NGOs, Northern governments'. *Voluntas*, 5.2, 155–92.

Steiner, M. (1996) *Developing the Global Teacher*. Stoke-on-Trent:Trentham.

Walker, G. (2006) *Educating the Global Citizen*. Saxmundham: John Catt.

2 Why global learning and global education? An educational approach influenced by the perspectives of Immanuel Kant[1]

Annette Scheunpflug

Introduction

There are various reasons to implement Global Learning and Global Education[2] within education. Vanessa Andreotti has elaborated the importance of global education in improving global social justice (see Chapter 4 in this volume). In this chapter I complement this perspective of global social justice by approaching the issues from the perspective of education and of the learner. First, I will address the question 'Why global learning and education?' using an educational approach; second, I outline some perspectives for the teaching methodology and the practice of global learning and education; and, third, I finish with some reflections regarding global learning and education theory and research.

Why global learning and education?

A starting point is the recognition that people need to have the knowledge and skills to live in a globalised world. They need to:

- be able to deal with the challenges of the globalised world, such as poverty, wealth, peace and participation (see e.g. UNDP 1999);

- engage with the uncertainty brought about by the acceleration of social change and by the fragmentation and hybridisation of cultures and lifestyles (see e.g. Appadurai 1990); and

- be able to engage in 'perspectives for change' and to have empathy for people they do not know, 'the other' (see e.g. Bourn 2001).

In summary, therefore, the first rationale for global education and learning is that it is necessary to prepare people to live in a more and more globalised world, in a way that enables them to respond to the challenges of an interconnected world, to take responsibility for, and to advocate for, global solidarity and social justice (see Scheunpflug 2003; Asbrand and Scheunpflug 2006).

These simple points however have far-reaching consequences. What does it mean to educate in ways that adequately address these challenges of global social justice?

Here I wish to move from the simple and obvious to provide a more philosophical foundation for global learning and education, in particular through the work of the German philosopher Immanuel Kant. In his 'Idea for a Universal History with a Cosmopolitan Purpose' (1964a), Kant based his ideas of a global world society on the consideration that human beings should not have any other option but to achieve global justice. In his thinking, global social justice is a universal obligation.

The challenge for the achievement of such a just world society, according to Kant, is to determine how a human being, necessarily thought of as a free person, 'can procure a magistracy which can maintain public justice and which is itself just' or, in my words, 'could become an advocate of public social justice in a way which would be just in and of itself' (Kant 1964a: A 397; translation by AS). In other words, the central question is how to respect human freedom, the freedom of the learner, and at the same time to move towards greater global solidarity and justice, enhancing the freedom of all, without diminishing the freedom of the learner, the human subject.

Using these insights from Kant from a political perspective, the question should be: 'How can the freedom of the individual be balanced with the freedom of the other?' Kant referred to this question in the area of the responsibility of politics, which he discussed in detail in 'Idea for a Universal History', but also in his considerations in 'Towards Perpetual Peace' (1964b). From the educational perspective, however, the question should possibly be: 'How to teach (global social justice) responsibility through education, if education does mean to constrain?'

Kant discussed this question in his tract 'On Education' (1900). For Kant it is essential to teach 'mankind's exit from its self-imposed immaturity' or, in other words, the overcoming of human beings' own immaturity (Kant 1996: 58). For Kant, it is essential that an adolescent should learn to access his reason 'without guidance from another',[3] that is to be educated to be a free, self-determined world citizen, responding to the needs of others, and who autonomously decides to live in a way that responds to the needs of others.

Kant gave the following answer to this question by stating that for education to enable the creation of autonomous and responsible world citizens, human beings needed to be treated in a way that assumes autonomy, global citizenship and responsibility. The autonomous subject, the global educated person, the model towards which human beings should be educated – the possibility of being such a subject has to be presupposed by such an education. Kant explains education in this paradoxical manner:[4] the *medium of education and the intended result of education* should be the same. Global learning and education, recognising global social justice, has at the same time to presuppose the freedom of the world citizen in the education process.

Implications for the practice of global learning and education

This philosophical perspective on global learning and education has implications for the theory and practice of global learning and education.[5] The aim now is to summarise these implications and to pose questions for further debate and research.

Implication 1: The need to maintain freedom

Activists, NGOs and those of us who are devoted to the political rationale for global learning and education might be tempted to draw political conclusions or make decisions regarding action or choices on behalf of students of global learning and education. This is a mistake, both strategically and educationally. Global learning and education requires that educators treat learners as fully emerging world citizens who come to autonomous decisions (for example for or against genetic seeds, for or against special agreements in the World Trade Organisation (WTO), for or against raising school enrolment in different countries, for or against regulation of debts and so on). Global learning and education should not hinder the 'forming of an independent judgement'. The borderline between global learning and education and indoctrination is located right at this point. Indoctrination is incompatible with an educator's (or indeed an NGO's or activist's) role in education in a democratic society.

For example many involved in development and global education are committed to the inclusion of certain forms of action within the educational process. But what type of action? Not all action proposed that has a relationship to campaigning is educational. Some actions are, but some are non-educational, and some can be perceived as mis-educational.

During the introduction of any political action into an educational process, the practice of freedom must prevail; otherwise it runs counter to the perspective of global learning and education outlined above. Unless the learner is involved in deciding the type of action, freely, as

21

part of the process, then it is not global learning or education. The NGO, activist or educator should not be the one deciding which politician to write to, which brand of fairly traded coffee to drink, which project to support, which protest to join. That is the job of the learner, in freedom, following choice. The educator may lead towards a menu of choices of actions relevant to particular learning, but the learner must choose. This is the only way that global learning for greater global justice and solidarity can ensue.

For example in Germany there was a state-wide activity in global learning during the Football World Cup in 2006. Classes in schools could choose any country from all over the world and qualify for the championship. The qualifying process was to present the country, to describe a learning process and to play a football game. Some 150 schools joined the championship and it was Angola, presented by a class from Potsdam, which won the game.

And that is why initiatives like One World Week in the UK are so interesting from a global education perspective – because learners are part of the process of deciding what should be learnt, what should be done and what should be acted upon, from a series of differing choices and perspectives.

Implication 2: Controversy must remain controversial

In global learning and education discourse there may be a consensus about the vision: a world of greater social justice. But how to reach this objective raises a range of difficult and controversial matters. It is suggested here that it is important that these controversies remain controversial.

I offer an example from Germany. In 2003 we analysed some teacher materials, from NGOs, for use in youth work and school settings, focused on TRIPS (Treatment of Intellectual Properties) within the then forthcoming WTO agreements. This was the central theme of the youth campaign on global education of the Catholic youth association and more than two million young people were asked to participate.

In this campaign, only a single aspect of TRIPS – the issue of bio-piracy and the advantage to multinational seed companies of the WTO agreement – was dealt with. While this is of course an important issue, there was no mention of other issues, or the more general dangers *and* challenges for third world countries within the teacher materials to support these activities. Complex themes and issues were reduced to simple and caricatured messages. Barbara Asbrand (see Chapter 3 in this volume) has shown in her study regarding young people's views of globalisation that young people are distrustful of this kind of information.

Global learning and education undertaken in this manner, far from engendering commitment, may, on the contrary, contribute to young people's distrust of political institutions. Instead, global learning and education should take the freedom of world citizens seriously and give them the possibility to vote for themselves as responsible subjects.

There are good examples from many NGOs of covering controversial topics. In a recent campaign by *Brot für die Welt* (Bread for the World) in Germany, for instance, worksheets were designed to give students the opportunity of exploring controversial issues and taking a range of actions. This perspective includes the acceptance that students may choose another position than would be expected from somebody convinced of the necessity of global social justice. Global learning and education requires a consensus on the legitimacy of dissent, or, put differently, on the necessity of a multiplicity of perspectives.

Result: A model of the ideal typical differentiation between global learning and education, lobbying and development information

In my experience, in order for NGOs to have the courage to enable students to discuss different perspectives on controversial issues, or to explore differing ways of achieving global social justice, they need a clear understanding regarding which part of their work is global learning and education and which part is lobbying and campaigning (see Table 2.1, although in practice the parts are more interlinked).

Table 2.1 Global education, lobbying and development information in a heuristic, ideal-typical differentiation

	Global education	Lobbying	Information
Why? **Legitimation**	Changing individuals (Development of free subjects; learning needs)	Changing politics	Changing deficits of knowledge
What? **Objective**	To enable people to live in a world society Understanding social justice	Publicity and advocacy for social justice	Communication about the work of organisations
How? **Didactics**	Learning as focus: – the prohibition against overwhelming – controversy must remain controversial – reproduction of social plurality	Engagement in campaigning and action	Giving information

In practice, it is sometimes difficult to distinguish these differences. When global learning and education is succeeding, people engage in fair trade or in campaigning and advocacy work. In this respect global learning and education is linked to lobbying and advocacy work. Global learning and education needs information and therefore it is linked to development information work. And in the practice of many NGOs, the three dimensions are linked together, often in one department, maintained by the same person.

But from time to time it is helpful to differentiate between the three, and not to forget the paradoxical character of global learning and education that leads to the freedom of the autonomous subject by treating them as autonomous world citizens, as Kant described.

Implications for theory and research

These perspectives also have implications for theory and research on global learning and education.

- We need a clear theoretical framework about the limitations of the freedom of the learner in global education. Does he or she have the right to decide against global social justice? If we stay with Kant's perspective we would say 'No'. But we have no consensus on where the borderline between a decision against global social justice and different ways to achieve global social justice is located. We have no didactical theory to work on these limitations. For example in adaptation of the educational position of Paulo Freire to a social perspective where the oppressor is hidden or even gone, liberation through education becomes more complex. Nevertheless, this recognition could help us to arrive at a more complex and less naive theory of global education.

- We need to understand better the anthropological and psychological foundations of global learning and education. Why should people agree, for their own purpose, to global education? Why do they resist moving towards greater global social justice? We need to learn more about the conditions for global solidarity, and people's chosen commitment to global social justice, using empirical research.

- We need to learn more about the effectiveness of the learning arrangements for global education. What competencies do people need to understand and move towards more global social justice? Which learning arrangements have consequences for global social justice? What could be the specific contribution of schools and NGOs in this field?

It is clear that global learning and global education are important for people and for the world. Improvement and innovation in any field important to human endeavour and to the future of the planet require research. But if we consider the importance of global learning to people and the world, and look then at the meagre amount of research pursued, supported or achieved in global education, it is something of an understatement to say that global education is really under-researched.

Conclusion

This chapter has aimed to demonstrate that global learning and education are essential for people to understand the globalised world in which they are living. But key to the global learning and education approach is the recognition of the Kantian concepts of freedom in order to become world citizens; practice needs to recognise this and not just give one perspective. Therefore key to future debates on global learning and education is the need to recognise the distinctions between information, awareness raising, learning and advocacy. These issues however lead onto wider questions about processes of learning, the limitations on this learning, psychological and anthropological foundations and the competencies people need to move forward towards global social justice.

Notes
1 I thank Liam Wegimont, Dublin, for some very helpful comments on this chapter.
2 In this chapter, I will use the term 'Global Learning' (the German notion) and 'Global Education' (the UK notion) synonymously.
3 See the correct quotation: 'Immaturity is the inability to make use of one's own understanding without the guidance of another. This immaturity is self-imposed when its cause lies not in lack of understanding, but in lack of resolve and courage to use it without guidance from another' (Kant 1996: 58).
4 In the words of Kant: 'One of the greatest problems of education is how to unite submission to the necessary *restraint* with the child's capability of exercising

his *freewill* – for restraint is necessary. How am I to develop the sense of freedom in spite of the restraint? I am to accustom my pupil to endure a restraint of his freedom, and at the same time I am to guide him to use his freedom aright' (Kant 1900: A33).

5 These implications were first formulated in Germany in 1977 as 'Beutelsbacher Konsens of political education' (see Wehling 1977; Sander 2004) for citizenship education, but for a long time did not resonate in global learning.

References

Appadurai, A. (1990) 'Disjuncture and difference in the global culture economy'. In M. Featherstone (ed.), *Global Culture: Nationalism, globalization and modernity*. London: Sage.

Asbrand, B. and Scheunpflug, A. (2006) 'Global education and education for sustainability'. *Environmental Education Research*, 12.1, 33–47.

Bourn, D. (2001) 'Global perspectives in lifelong learning'. *Research in Post-Compulsory Education*, 6.3, 325–38.

Kant, I. (1900) On Education [Über Paedagogik], translated by Annette Churton, introduction by C.A. Foley Rhys Davids. Boston: D.C. Heath and Co.

—— (1996) An Answer to the Question: What is Enlightenment? [Beantwortung der Frage, was ist Aufklärung?], translated by James Schmidt. In James Schmidt (ed.), *What is Enlightenment?* Berkeley: University of California Press.

—— (1964a) Idee zu einer allgemeinen Geschichte in weltbürgerlicher Absicht [Idea for a Universal History with a Cosmopolitan Purpose]. *Kant Studienausgabe*, Vol. VI, edited by W. Weischedel. Darmstadt.

—— (1964b) Zum ewigen Frieden. Ein philosophischer Entwurf [Perpetual Peace]. *Kant Studienausgabe*, Vol. VI, edited by W. Weischedel. Darmstadt.

Sander, W. (2004) 'Incitement to freedom: competencies of political education in a world of difference', *Development Education Journal*, 11.1, 9–11.

Scheunpflug, A. (2003) Stichwort: Globalisierung und Erziehungswissenschaft. *Zeitschrift für Erziehungswissenschaft*, 6. Jahrgang, Heft 2, 159–72.

United Nations Development Program (UNDP) (1999) *Bericht über die menschliche Entwicklung: Globalisierung mit menschlichem Antlitz.* [Human development report], Bonn: Deutschen Gesellschaft für die Vereinten Nationen e.V.

Wehling, H.-G. (1977) 'Konsens à la Beutelsbach?' In S. Schiele and H. Schneider (eds), *Das Konsensproblem in der politischen Bildung*. Stuttgart.

3 How adolescents learn about globalisation and development

Barbara Asbrand

Introduction

How young people learn about globalisation and development is the theme of this chapter. It is based on the outcomes of a major research project in Germany. The focus is on young people's knowledge about the world and their ability to act in a world society (Asbrand 2006). It covers two major themes that have emerged from the research in terms of how young people relate to understanding global questions:

- strategies to reduce complexity within learning environments; and

- different ways that uncertainty is dealt with, depending on gender.

The chapter summarises the issues to emerge from the research and poses some questions as to the need for further research.

Why focus on complexity and uncertainty?

According to the research conducted, it was found that the most important conditions in order to be able to act in a globalised world are adequate strategies for reducing complexity and uncertainty (Asbrand

2005). Put another way, developing a strategy for the reduction of complexity can be seen as the most important competency within global education. The main objective of global education is to provide learners with competencies to live in a world society and to shape this complex, globalised world in terms of a just and sustainable future (Scheunpflug and Schröck 2002; Scheunpflug 2003; Asbrand and Scheunpflug 2006). These competencies first require the ability to act. Learners have to develop a positive attitude regarding the possibilities of acting in a globalised world. If they experience only the uncertainty and complexity of the global world, they may be discouraged from acting responsibly to shape a just and sustainable future. So the competency to deal with complexity has to be a central aim of global education.

Before moving on to consider the results of the research, particularly concerning the ability to act in a world society, here is an outline of the design of the research.

Research question

The understanding of globalisation in this chapter is based on the theory of world society of the German sociologist Niklas Luhmann (1997). Luhmann holds that the most important characteristic of world society is an increasing uncertainty about the future. This becomes obvious when we consider many current societal trends:

- the risk of unemployment;
- climate change and other environmental problems;
- increasing political insecurity in many regions of the world; and
- the fact that neither politicians nor academics provide clear and obvious solutions for these types of problems.

The second characteristic of world society, according to Luhmann, is the seemingly contradictory phenomenon of the increase of knowledge, on the one hand, and the increase of 'non-knowledge' or 'unknowability', on the other hand (Luhmann 1997: 149). Young people in today's world are aware of these insecurities and uncertainties. This is can also be seen very clearly in the group discussions undertaken with adolescents during the research.

The research question of the project was: How do adolescents create their knowledge about the world? Underlying this question is the assumption that knowledge is socially constructed. This question leads to two further questions:

1   What are the world views and ideas of adolescents about global perspectives?

2   In which ways do they deal with the complexity of world society?

The idea of the research was to investigate knowledge about the world and the world views of learners, and in particular to reconstruct the genesis of knowledge or learning processes. The interest of the research was to learn more about how learning processes function. The research assumed that a structural description of learning processes, focused on global understanding, would yield fruitful conclusions for the theory and practice of global education.

Methodology

The main themes of this chapter – 'strategies to reduce complexity within the learning environments' and 'different ways of dealing with uncertainty depending on gender' – make clear that comparative analysis is of utmost importance in the qualitative methodology used in the research project. This methodology, called the documentary method (Bohnsack 2003), is based on the sociology of knowledge following the approach of Karl Mannheim (1964, 1980; see Bohnsack 2003). During the interpretation of the qualitative data, a typology was developed which aims to explain the different orientations of adolescents according to fundamental experiences like social and cultural environment and social background; and socialisation, such as gender-specific experiences. In this chapter the results are presented that emerged from the comparative analysis of different learning environments, such as:

- school lessons;
- school-based extra-curricular activities; and
- non-formal youth work outside school.

The documentary method is based on the assumption that specific orientations, world views or knowledge are framed by fundamental experiences of specific social surroundings or environments. The results of the research project show indeed that the structure of the learning arrangement constitutes specific experiences that shape the orientations and knowledge of learners. In this chapter strategies to reduce complexity depending on the learning environment are therefore described first, and then different ways of dealing with uncertainty depending on gender are outlined. Gender-specific experiences can also be seen as fundamental experiences which obviously lead to different world views of female and male adolescents.

For the inquiry, this qualitative research used the group discussion method (Bohnsack 2003; Loos and Schäffer 2001). The idea of this approach is that the participants can express what is important to them; they do not answer questions formulated in advance by the researcher, but have the chance to express their point of view with little or no influence from predetermined questions.

Group discussions were conducted with different groups of adolescents. Most participants were 17–19 years old. There were three major groups, which are compared in the analysis:

- pupils learning about global issues in school lessons (religious education, civic education, foreign languages);

- pupils participating in school-based extra-curricular activities in global education space (e.g. Fair Trade projects, international school partnerships); and

- young people involved in the activities of NGOs and youth organisations outside school, for example young people volunteering in the youth organisation of trade unions or within an environmental organisation.

The qualitative data was analysed by means of the documentary method, following Ralf Bohnsack (2003). The aim of using this methodology is the description of patterns of orientation and description of learning processes. Like the underlying theoretical framework of system-theory, the theoretical background of this methodology is a constructivist understanding of knowledge.

Using the documentary method, the following steps of interpretation are carried out. First, the analysis of the discussion aims to describe what the participants are talking about and, second, how they discuss the issues. Differentiation between content of the discussion and the ways of discussing it is based on the distinction between explicit and tacit knowledge. Explicit knowledge corresponds to *what* the participants talk about in the group discussion. The methodology, based on the theory of Karl Mannheim (1964; 1980), works on the assumption that an analysis of *how* an issue is discussed will provide evidence of the tacit knowledge of the group, which can then be described. Bohnsack, following Mannheim, assumes that in this kind of knowledge implicit patterns of fundamental orientation frame the practice and the behaviour of people (2003: 59). This is not understood as intentional action, but as a habitual practice shaped by tacit knowledge and implicit patterns. As already mentioned, tacit knowledge, according to the assumptions of the methodology, is based on fundamental, constitutive experiences, like different social and cultural backgrounds, milieus or socialisation such as gender-specific experiences.

The next important step of interpretation in this research, according to the documentary method, is comparative analysis (Bohnsack 2003: 135ff.). By comparing, for example, the knowledge and the orientation of pupils who encountered issues of global education in school lessons with the knowledge and orientation of adolescents who dealt with the issue in youth work, voluntarily and outside school, the characteristics of both particular learning environments can be worked out. This step of interpretation, this comparing, leads to the development of a typology based on the comparative analysis of empirical cases.

In this chapter some results of the qualitative analysis are outlined in the following sections.

Strategies for the reduction of complexity depending on the learning environment

The first example is the orientation of students, in particular pupils of grammar schools, which was reconstructed in comparison with adolescents volunteering outside school. Following the system-theory of Luhmann this can be described as 'moral communication' (Luhmann 1987: 317ff, 1990). To illustrate the interpretation, the first example is from a group discussion with pupils of a grammar school, who were involved in global education in civic education.[1]

> Am: Well, if you look at the products, for example, if I think of Nike sportshoes for example, usually they are produced under conditions. Well, since I have realised that the workers earn just a little money and since I have learned about the working-conditions, and so on, I don't know, this kind of products, those products with a popular brand-name they became somehow something dirty.

> Bf: I mean we have talked about child-labour, for example carpets are made by children, and sometimes also sportshoes; and if

you know about that, then you think twice, no you think ten
times, if you should buy the shoes or not.

In this short excerpt of the group discussion the students are talking
about the possibility of ethical consumption. The discussion shows that
values of ethical consumption were obviously an issue of the lessons:
Bf says 'we have talked about'. Second, the discussion shows that the
values are shared by the adolescents. Bf says that she thinks through
the problem of bad working conditions since she has learned about it.
So far, we can say that if the objective of global education is to teach
an ethical orientation in the sense of justice and sustainability, then in
this case obviously the objective is achieved. Pupils think of aspects of
social and ethical standards in a global perspective when they are
discussing their patterns of consumption. The discussion continued as
follows:

?f: (there is no other choice).

?f: ⌊ (yes, of course…).

Gf: You just can get shoes made by children

?f: ⌊ (sportshoes)

Bf: ⌊ I mean most of them
      are made by children

Gf: ⌊ you can't walk barefooted –

?f: ⌊ yes, of course

Bf: Well, in any case you have to buy something even if you don't

?f: ⌊ (because the market offers only these sportshoes)

Bf: want to support child-labour, but there is no other choice

?f: yes, exactly.

Am: yeah. (2)

Df: Most of the people buy these things, like Nike shoes, everyone
      wants to have them. Therefore they are bought.

Am: That's the way it is.

Now the group of students discusses why they can't put these ethical values into practice. They are discussing different relevant arguments beside moral aspects, such as fashion and the market. They recognise the fact that products that cover the criteria of ethical consumption are not available. The pupils observe the fact that in their day-to-day life ethical consumption is not a common practice. Everyone is used to buying Nike shoes. This discourse seems to be a strategy for excusing the fact that the adolescents do not act according to the values discussed in the civic education lessons. In the case of this group of pupils, moral communication does not lead to action, although there is a serious discussion of the values and issues taught in global education. The issue of ethical consumption is discussed in terms of a moral problem and there is serious reflection in this discussion by adolescents. Therefore one cannot say that they do not care about the global perspective. But in their daily lives it is not often possible for them to put their values into practice.

In the discussions of these grammar school students there is a lot of intellectual activity, of reflection and thinking about options to act, but they are not practical, they are just thought through theoretically. These discussions document an orientation which is typical of the grammar school students in our research. It is based on the recognition of different perspectives, and on a reflection regarding non-knowledge. It is based in the typical activity of grammar school lessons, the quest for knowledge, which includes the awareness of non-knowledge too. These grammar school students achieve an extensive knowledge but that intellectual activity leads not to certainty in regard to the ability to act but to scepticism. Any knowledge is queried, because the recognition of the fact of non-knowledge includes the awareness of the contingency of any knowledge. Students are very critical about the authenticity and the truth of such knowledge and are always considering alternatives or potential possibilities that theoretically could exist. In the end the knowledge that is taught in school lessons remains theoretical. It does not become relevant to the practice of young people, although their attitudes towards values like international justice and sustainability is beyond doubt.

One of the very important findings of the research is this difference between attitudes and values, which are shared theoretically, and the ability to act in a world society which seems to be less dependent on the intentions and ideas of justice, but rather related to strategies of reduction of complexity. The example shows that moral communication is not an adequate strategy to achieve the competency to act in the globalised world (see Luhmann 1990).

The described reconstruction of this orientation of pupils was developed through a comparative analysis with groups of adolescents in non-formal youth work. Compared with the learning processes which took place in a school environment the construction of knowledge of young people outside school is different: the strategy of reduction of complexity can be described as absorption of uncertainty through organisations. This analysis again draws heavily on the systems-theory of Niklas Luhmann (1997: 826ff, 2000). Compared with the uncertainty of the school pupils researched, the knowledge of the young people involved in activities outside school is relatively secure. They feel certain about their knowledge and there is no consideration of non-knowledge or different perspectives. This knowledge therefore is termed a 'metastory' (Luhmann 1987) which implies that the knowledge of the group is not doubted and the truth of the knowledge is not questioned. A group of young people volunteering in the Attac network, for example, are clear that from their point of view globalisation is unjust, and they know precisely that it is and why they think it is. There is no doubt in their minds about that.

As a consequence of the secure knowledge of the people in the group, committed as they are to other world views, other people – even friends of group members – are excluded, and deemed to be uninformed or ignorant. This phenomenon can be observed in all the groups of adolescents volunteering outside school which were investigated in the research project. The process of exclusion typical of the youth groups in non-formal youth work becomes evident in comparison with the groups of school pupils in the sample of this research project, where it does not happen.

The knowledge of adolescents volunteering in organisations outside school, which is taken as true and objective, leads to a value-based orientation and clarity about possibilities to act in a world society. This enables adolescents to be active and facilitates the ability to act. This secure knowledge, which corresponds to the characteristics of an undoubted and unquestioned metastory, in all cases of youth groups outside school, is similar to the programmes of the organisation that the young people belong to. This strategy of reduction of complexity Luhmann calls 'absorption of uncertainty through organisation' (1997: 826ff.). The affiliation to the organisation, which is of utmost importance to the groups, leads to certainty regarding knowledge and regarding the options of acting in a complex world society.

There is an obvious connection between secure knowledge, a self-image of being active and an optimistic world view as well, although this knowledge is certainly somehow undifferentiated and excluding. Compared with this orientation, the intellectual practice of school pupils, reflecting different perspectives and the contingency of world views, becomes obvious in the comparative analysis.

Different ways of dealing with uncertainty depending on gender

A gender-specific typology regarding different ways of dealing with uncertainty will be outlined on the basis of an example of a school where group discussions were held with both female and male groups of pupils. All the pupils attend the same grammar school and the same classes and are around 18 years old. The special characteristic of the school is that there is a World Shop run as a mini-company by the pupils, called 'a pupils' company'. This means that a group of volunteers – working together with teachers – run a shop where they sell Fair Trade products. The objective of this kind of extra-curricular project, which has recently become popular in Germany, is to enable pupils to acquire competencies and skills such as teamwork, project management, communication skills and so on. The project has a secondary objective: to facilitate learning about global issues. The experience gained in the pupils' company is usually accompanied by systematic instruction in classes. The only difference between the female and the male groups is that the female pupils volunteer to work in the pupils' company and the male pupils do not. The members of both groups experienced the same school lessons. Due to the fact that the activities of the World Shop run by the pupils' company are very present in that school and because the young men deal with the issue of Fair Trade in the lessons too, the young men are informed about Fair Trade, although they do not participate in the extra-curricular project of the World Shop as the young women do. By comparing the implicit frames of knowledge of groups of female and male adolescents in the research a typology of gender concerning ways of dealing with complexity evolved.

The following extract is from the group discussion with male adolescents and reports the discussion of the young men about the reliability of the Fair Trade label.

> Am: To be honest, I believe almost everything, anyway, but the problem is nonetheless one can't be totally sure that everything is all right with the Fairtrade mark. If they state, if they put the label on the product, where do I get the knowledge from? Like it is with the bio-label, where they put the bio-label on organic cheese. Anyway, they say that the Fairtrade mark guarantees that there is no child labour, and appropriate wages are paid so that they can have a proper life, but from where should I know that there is no corruption within Fairtrade too? Well, that can happen there likewise. That's the problem that I don't know surely. Anyhow, who confirms that the whole thing of Fairtrade runs in the right way?

> Bm: I don't know.

This example shows the importance of certainty and the need for security in the young men's orientation. It is an example of the strategy to reduce complexity by balancing the risks (Luhmann 1990). Under the condition of uncertainty and complexity of the world society any action is risky, because the effect of an action is not predictable. The young men in this example are discussing the suspected effects of a potential action – in this case the consumption of Fair Trade products. In this discussion they mistrust the impact of Fair Trade; because – in their view – there exists no secure knowledge about the question of whether Fair Trade labelling is functioning in the right way, the effect of action is not secure. In consequence the young men are not aware of the risk, but they choose the secure way, which means – in the face of insecurity – not to act. They prefer to remain passive, because the effects of action are not secure and not foreseeable.

This implicit orientation of the young men can be termed as an *instrumental orientation*. Value-based action to them is meaningful only when a benefit or the achievement of objectives is foreseeable. The ability to act of the young men is oriented to utility; the meaning of acting is dependent on the assessment of the results of action and the achievement of purposes, so action is determined by cost-benefit considerations. But under the condition of uncertainty the achievement of impact is unsure and the young men's competency to act is therefore limited. Different models of action in the context of development education, not only the model of Fair Trade but also the activities of charities or development cooperation, are perceived sceptically by the male adolescents. Their perceptions of the future are sceptical in general and their attitudes towards acting are shaped by passivity. They do not deem value-based action in relation to global issues to be feasible.

In comparison, the essential characteristic of the self-image described by the young women is that of *being active*. The following example is from discussion with the female group who volunteer in the pupils' company. The extract follows the question of the researcher as to why the young women spend their leisure time working in a project at school. In the previous part of the discussion they had described in detail how they work together in the pupils' company. This discourse documents the fact that this practice, which the young women share with others, is crucially important to them. It is a practice they share with other young people of their peer group. As is mentioned briefly in this example, they were also occupied with all the responsible and demanding tasks of the pupils' company, their self-image expressed in the group discussion is the role of management (being active). According to the pedagogical approach of pupils' companies, the practice within the pupils' company is the responsibility of the adolescents themselves, and is not determined by teachers. The job of the teachers is just to accompany the pupils.

> Y: And why have you joined the Fair Trade group as volunteers?

> Cf: Well, actually we asked this question ourselves quite often, but we didn't really find an answer. Well, in the beginning it was just for fun, I don't know it was simply something new. There were a lot of working groups offered at the school and we had been very curious, it was a new school and the main thing was to join one of these working groups. Well, first they decided to check out the World Shop, and then a bit at a time we all joined the Fair Trade group too, and afterwards it became sort of part of us. Everywhere and all the time we were talking about the World Shop, which products shall we order, how shall we organise this and that; well, that is just the way it was. And little by little we noticed that the whole matter is valuable, something worth to stand for instead of watching TV.

This example from the discussion of the young women shows that their main interest – at least at the beginning of their commitment to the Fair Trade group – was not dedicated to the objectives and intentions of Fair Trade such as the support of worldwide justice. The primary interest of the young women was to get to know other pupils when they started at a new school. The main objective was therefore to spend time together with other young people and to have fun. Then the shared practice became important, their identification with the group is so extensive that they feel that the activity is 'a part of' themselves. In the view expressed by the group, the purposes of Fair Trade in terms of supporting justice in worldwide trade are only of secondary importance. The experience, 'that the whole matter is something valuable', seems to be merely a pleasant side effect; it was by no means their intention in joining the Fair Trade group.

There is another important difference between male and female adolescents that might be added. Compared with the sceptical orientation of the young men, the girls are expressing an optimistic perspective on the future. In the orientation of the young women global justice is not just an ideal but something which somehow can be realised in the future – at least in a limited way.

In this example, the members of the female group appear competent to act in a global context. They seem to have the capability to act in a complex world society – without depending on a restricted world view like the young people belonging to organisations outside school. The female pupils share the reflected perspective on the variety, plurality and contingency of knowledge with their male colleagues. However, in contrast to their male colleagues, they obviously develop strategies for the reduction of complexity that leads to the ability to act under the condition of complexity in a globalised world. The orientation of the female adolescents therefore is termed a constructive way to deal with complexity. The fundamental experience that enables the young women to act responsibly in a globalised world is obviously a specific kind of practice, which appears for instance in the pupils' company. This practice, in my view, is distinguished by two specific characteristics.

1   In all groups where this phenomenon is observed the practice is a social context of a peer group. It is less influenced by adults but it is a shared activity of adolescents. The main intention is to meet others. And it is somehow a situational and to some extent spontaneous activity.

2   The practice is not oriented to a purpose and this seems to be the most important point. In other mixed groups investigated during the research the females do not contradict the proposition of the males that intentional action often does

not achieve its objectives in a globalised world. But to the girls, value-based action could be meaningful beyond the achievement of purposes. It has its end in itself – like in this example of the pupils' company. The decision to participate in the Fair Trade group did not depend on the purposes of Fair Trade, as the girls joined the group in the beginning just because of the social experience. It was later that the process of action itself became valuable.

These characteristics of action correspond with those distinguishing marks Bohnsack et al. describe as the actionism of young people (Bohnsack et al. 1995; Bohnsack and Nohl 2001, 2003). Psychologists call this experience the experience of self-impact (Edelstein 2001; Schwarzer and Jerusalem 2002; Nentwig-Gesemann et al. 2005). To enable the experience of self-impact, which is assumed to be a relevant aspect of learning in the context of ethical education, there is a need for serious practice, which allows impact in real life – which goes further than several action-centred learning approaches. In the example of the World Shop the girls gain the experience that their actions have an impact in real life, for example successful turnover in the pupils' company or responsibility for its management. The strategy of reduction of complexity in this case is based in the social relationships which the young women experience in this kind of action. They are able to rely on the experience of meaningful practice in the past and present, which enables confidence in the future. In this female orientation there is no need to provide security for the achievement of purposes. They are more likely to be able to act in the context of world society.

Conclusions

With these conclusions based on the empirical analysis, I can move from empirical description to considerations in regard to the further development of the concept of global education.

The first conclusion, drawn from the moral discussions of the school pupils, is that global education in my opinion does not have to teach specific values, but the teaching should aim to enable young people to find their own opinions, to enable them to acquire competencies of moral judgement. For this reason the teaching of ethical issues has to be analysed critically to see if it promotes reflection on ethical or moral values and attitudes or if it just teaches a specific moral point of view.

Second, global education, if it aims at competencies to act and to shape the global, can profit from serious and complex practice in the social context of a peer group, which allows experience of self-impact. In order to avoid the development of an undifferentiated world view by pupils, accompanying pedagogical support and systematic instruction are essential at the same time – in schools and in youth work outside school as well.

Note
1 In the transcription m stands for male and f for female adolescents. A question mark indicates that the speaker is not to be identified. ⌊ indicates that two people are speaking at the same time.

References

Asbrand, Barbara (2005) Unsicherheit in der Globalisierung. Orientierungen von Jugendlichen in der Weltgesellschaft. *Zeitschrift für Erziehungswissenschaft*, 8. Jg. Heft 2, S. 223–39.

—— (2006) Orientierungen in der Weltgesellschaft. *Eine qualitativ-rekonstruktive Studie zur Konstruktion von Wissen und Handlungsorientierung von Jugendlichen in schulischen Lernarrangements und in der außerschulischen Jugendarbeit.* Habilitationsschrift Universität Erlangen-Nürnberg.

Asbrand, Barbara and Scheunpflug, Annette (2006), 'Global education and education for sustainability'. *Environmental Education Research*, 12.1, 33–46.

Bohnsack, Ralf (2003) Rekonstruktive Sozialforschung. Einführung in *Qualitative Methoden*. 5. Aufl. Opladen.

Bohnsack, Ralf and Nohl, Arnd-Michael (2001) Jugendkulturen und Aktionismus. Eine rekonstruktive empirische Analyse am Beispiel des Breakdance. In Hans Merkens and Jürgen Zinnecker (Hrsg.), *Jahrbuch Jugendforschung* 1. Opladen, S. 17–37.

Bohnsack, Ralf and Nohl, Arnd-Michael (2003) 'Youth culture as practical innovation. Turkish German youth, "time out" and the actionisms of breakdance'. *European Journal of Cultural Studies*, 6.3, 367–86.

Bohnsack, Ralf, Loos, Peter, Schäffer, Burkhard, Staedtler, Klaus and Wild, Bodo (1995) *Die Suche nach Gemeinsamkeit und die Gewalt der Gruppe. Hooligans, Musikgruppen und andere Jugendcliquen im Vergleich*. Opladen.

Edelstein, Wolfgang (2001) Gesellschaftliche Anomie und moralpädagogische Intervention. Moral im Zeitalter individueller Wirksamkeitserwartungen. In W. Edelstein, F.Oser and P. Schuster (Hrsg.), *Moralische Erziehung in der Schule*. Weinheim und Basel, S. 13–34.

Loos, Peter and Schäffer, Burkhard (2001) *Das Gruppendiskussionsverfahren*. Opladen.

Luhmann, Niklas (1987) *Soziale Systeme. Grundriss einer allgemeinen Theorie*. Frankfurt am Main.

—— (1990) *Paradigm lost: Über die ethische Reflexion der Moral*. Frankfurt am Main.

—— (1997) *Die Gesellschaft der Gesellschaft*. Frankfurt am Main.

—— (2000) *Organisation und Entscheidung*. Opladen/Wiesbaden.

Mannheim, Karl (1964) Beiträge zur Theorie der Weltanschauungsinterpretation. In Karl Mannheim, *Wissenssoziologie*. Berlin/Neuwied, S. 91–154.

—— (1980) *Strukturen des Denkens*. Frankfurt am Main. (Original: unpublished manuscript 1922–25).

Nentwig-Gesemann, Iris, Streblow, Claudia and Bohnsack, Ralf (2005) Schlüsselerlebnisse und Lernprozesse Jugendlicher in zukunftsqualifizierender Projektarbeit. Eine programmübergreifende Analyse. In Deutsche Kinder- und Jugendstiftung (Hrsg.), Jung Talentiert. *Chancenreich? Beschäftigungsfähigkeit von Jugendlichen fördern*. Opladen, S. 47–90.

Schwarzer, Rolf and Jerusalem, Matthias (2002) Das Konzept der Selbstwirksamkeit. *Zeitschrift für Pädagogik*, 44. Beiheft, S. 28–53.

Scheunpflug, Annette (2003) 'Education for sustainable development in Germany'. *Development Education Journal*, 9.3, 36–8.

Scheunpflug Annette and Schröck, Nikolaus (2002) Globales Lernen. Einführung in eine pädagogische Konzeption zur entwicklungsbezogenen Bildung. Hrsg. *Brot für die Welt*, 2. Aufl. Stuttgart.

4 Development vs poverty: notions of cultural supremacy in development education policy

Vanessa Andreotti

Introduction

In this chapter, I use a postcolonial theoretical framework based on the works of Homi Bhabha and Gayatri Spivak to examine notions of development and poverty in the curriculum guidance document 'Developing a Global Dimension in the School Curriculum' (DGDSC) published in 2000. I offer a situated analysis of how these notions can potentially affect learners' perceptions of the 'Global South'[1] and reinforce notions of cultural supremacy. I start with a description of the document followed by an analysis of the content focusing on the document's approach to poverty and development. I finish this chapter with a comparison between the conceptual framework of the document and that of a postcolonial perspective. This chapter draws on a broader study of discourses and practices related to the global dimension.

'Developing a Global Dimension in the School Curriculum' description: definitions, aims and justifications

DGDSC was produced by the former Central Bureau of the British Council and the Development Education Association (DEA), and first published by the Department for Education and Skills (DfES) in 2000. The booklet was updated by the DEA and reprinted in March 2005 with minor changes in structure. In this chapter, I analyse only the version of 2000, which was the main reference document for schools in relation to the global dimension in education in England from 2000 to 2004.

DGDSC offers three references to what it means to include the 'Global Dimension' (GD) in the curriculum and how it affects students:

> Including a global dimension in teaching means that links can be made between local and global issues and that what is taught is informed by international and global matters.
>
> (DfES 2000: 2)

> Including a global dimension means that the content of what is taught is informed by international and global matters, so preparing pupils to live their lives in a global society. It means addressing issues such as sustainable development, interdependence and social justice at both the local and global level.
>
> (DfES 2000: 1)

> It also means that young people are given opportunities to examine their own values and attitudes, to appreciate the similarities between peoples everywhere, to understand the global context of their local lives, and to develop skills that will enable them to combat prejudice and discrimination. This in turn gives young people the knowledge, skills and understanding to play an active role in the global community.
>
> (DfES 2000: 1)

DGDSC does not provide a clear definition or conceptualisation of what GD means, but from these assertions GD can be interpreted as the establishment of connections between local and global issues in a way that involves an examination of an individual's role in the world and of her values and attitudes. The values associated with GD can be read as related to combating prejudice and discrimination and to becoming an 'active citizen' in a 'global community'.

The booklet justifies GD on the basis of globalisation, which is defined as intensified trade, travel and communication across the world from the perspective of people who have access to such commodities:

> Global issues are part of young people's lives in a way that they never were for previous generations. Television, the internet, international sport and increased opportunities for travel, all bring the wider world into everyone's daily life.
>
> (DfES 2000: 2)

It portrays the intensified contact with cultural difference as a societal improvement that opens opportunities for broadening pupils' experience and knowledge:

> Society today is enhanced by peoples, cultures, languages, religions, art, technologies, music and literature originating in many different parts of the world. This provides a tremendous range of positive opportunities to broaden pupils' experience and knowledge.
>
> (DfES 2000: 2)

It conceives poverty as a lack of access to healthcare, water, education and opportunities for improvement and states that global environmental damage is worsened by poverty. Another reference to global processes is made in the assertion that:

> economies around the world are more than ever interdependent on both trade with, and investment from, other countries ... the importance of education in helping young people recognise their role and responsibilities as members of this global community is becoming increasingly apparent.
>
> (DfES 2000: 2)

The document states that the revised national curriculum provides more opportunities for the incorporation of GD in the 'work and life of schools' than the previous national curriculum. It identifies the statement about the values, aims and purposes of the curriculum that are related to GD and includes three quotations that justify the introduction of GD in the curriculum.

The first is related to the role of education in shaping individuals committed to equal opportunities, a liberal pluralist democracy and sustainable development.

> Education is ... a route to equality of opportunity for all, a healthy and just democracy, a productive economy, and sustainable development. Education should reflect the enduring values that contribute to these ends. These include valuing ... the wider groups to which we belong, the diversity in our society and the environment in which we live.... The school curriculum ... should secure commitment to sustainable development at a personal, national and global level.
>
> (QCA 1999: 1, cited in DfES 2000: 2)

The second is related to communication and the changing nature of society due to globalising forces acting upon the economy and society and the expansion of communication technologies that change work and leisure patterns:

> education must enable us to respond positively to the opportunities and challenges of the rapidly changing world in which we live and work ... we need to be prepared to engage as individuals, parents, workers and citizens with economic, social and cultural change, including the continued globalisation of the economy and society, with new work and leisure patterns and with the rapid expansion of communication technologies.
>
> (QCA 1999: 1, cited in DfES 2000: 2)

The third statement is related to the construction of pupils' identities, of cultural heritages of British society and of different geographical dimensions of their lives:

> The school curriculum should contribute to the development of pupils' sense of identity through knowledge and understanding of the spiritual, moral, social and cultural heritages of Britain's diverse society and of the local, national, European, Commonwealth and global dimensions of their lives.
>
> (QCA 1999: 1, cited in DfES 2000: 3)

The document also offers a progression for the four key stages. Key stages 1 and 2 focus primarily on identity, diversity and the development of a sense of common humanity 'with similar needs but differences in how these needs are met' (DfES 2000: 3). Disparities in the world and notions of social justice and interdependence are introduced in key stage 2 and developed in key stages 3 and 4. It is only in key stages 3 and 4 that critical thinking and poverty are mentioned.

The document outlines eight key concepts underpinning teaching about global issues. These are: citizenship, sustainable development, social justice, values and perceptions, diversity, interdependence, conflict resolution and human rights (DfES 2000).

For each key stage and also for the key concepts, the DGDSC offers guidelines for each subject with 15 case studies offering examples of good practice.

Four of the case studies illustrate links between schools in England and schools in developing countries and a special section at the end of the document is dedicated to school linking, which is justified primarily as way to enrich the life of schools, to offer opportunity for research and knowledge exchange and to 'bring issues vividly to life' (DfES 2000: 14). Another justification given for linking is that it offers an opportunity to open subject areas to add 'wider global input and perspectives' (ibid.). It is also stated that:

> exchanging ideas with teachers and pupils on an equal basis,
> whether it is about science, environmental issues, the arts, or culture,
> can challenge the stereotyped, 'problem oriented' image of people
> in less affluent countries and thereby contributes to education in
> values and attitudes in a multicultural global society.
>
> (DfES 2000: 14)

However, what is meant by 'equal' or how an 'equal partnership' with a 'less affluent country' can be established are issues that are not addressed in the guidelines.

DGDSC also offers a special section on whole school approaches (or approaches that involve the whole school as opposed to isolated disciplines) which features examples like 'international school days', school clusters working together and the involvement of parents, organisations and the wider community to 'contribute their knowledge and experience of the wider world in assemblies and as part of classroom discussions' (DfES 2000: 15).

Internet links and addresses directing readers to materials, resources and organisations are listed at the end of the document together with quotations from educators on the perceived value of GD.

Content analysis

The way the document defines what the introduction of GD in the curriculum means puts an emphasis on making links between local and global contexts and the inclusion of 'international matters', which, from the information in the links section, can also be understood as international perspectives. It also stresses the creation of opportunities for pupils in the UK to examine their own values and attitudes, exemplified in the idea of challenging discrimination and stereotypes and critical assessment of information (in KS3), to develop an appreciation for diversity and to build the knowledge, understanding and skills to become active citizens in a global society. This definition foregrounds the content (i.e. connections between local and global contexts) and methodology of GD (i.e. incorporating different perspectives and assessing information critically).

However, the epistemology presented in the document contradicts some of these principles as the text presents a complex juxtaposition of two different sets of assumptions: a liberal multiculturalist view of diversity, identity and culture, and a dominant modernisation approach to development and poverty with very few traces of the alternative and the dependency school approaches to development. Neither the approach to culture, nor the approach to poverty and development challenge the ideas of a linear collective history and of a seamless narrative of progress, which are questioned in both post-development and postcolonial perspectives. The implication of this is that, in DGDSC there is only one version of reality that is considered legitimate (neutral and objective) 'knowledge' – other knowledges, rationalities and logics are framed as 'values, beliefs and traditions' (Andreotti 2006a). Thus, from a postcolonial perspective both discourses identified operate within Eurocentric-universalising epistemologies that tend to reinforce notions of cultural supremacy.

The approach to development and poverty

The approach to development and poverty in the document is based on the modernisation approach to development with traces of other approaches. Within the modernisation approach the Third World is at a backward stage according to the economic parameters established by the 'First World' and needs First World assistance to modernise and grow economically through the rational use of resources brought by Western modes of organisation, science and technology (Sylvester 1999). The focus of this approach is on economic growth and 'progress' defined in relation to 'Northern' parameters.

The document seems to be addressing a context of assumed political apathy and indifference in relation to poverty. This can be observed in the document's emphasis on 'active citizenship':

> At key stages 3 and 4 pupils develop their understanding of their role as global citizens and extend their knowledge of the wider world. Their understanding of issues such as poverty, social justice and sustainable development increases *and they realise the importance of taking action to improve the world for future generations.*
>
> (DfES 2000: 3)

> Citizenship: Gaining the knowledge, skills and understanding necessary to become informed, *active*, responsible *global citizens.*
>
> (DfES 2000: 8)

History: explaining the role of national and international
organisations throughout history; highlighting different forms of
action to effect change.

(DfES 2000: 8)

Citizenship: teaching about democratic institutions and different
political and societal structures; encouraging pupils to participate
and become *active citizens.*

(DfES 2000: 8)

This discourse of active global citizenship is based on the premise that
individuals have a moral responsibility towards others based on their
'position in the world' and (resulting) capacity to affect global
processes, or 'the future of the planet and its people':

At key stage 2 pupils develop their understanding beyond their own
experience.... They develop their sense of social justice and *moral
responsibility and begin to understand that their own choices can
affect global issues as well as local ones.*

(DfES 2000: 3)

RE: teaching about the moral and social obligations we have towards
each other.

(DfES 2000: 9)

Geography: inspiring pupils to think about their own place in the
world and their rights and responsibilities to other people.

(DfES 2000: 8)

Citizenship: showing how pupils can become citizens making a
contribution to the future well-being of the planet and its people.

(DfES 2000: 8)

However, depending on how development and well-being are defined,
this moral responsibility can take different forms and imply different
assumptions about the role of the North in relation to the South.

In the document, societal improvements are associated with development, technology, global trade and 'quality of life':

> Geography: showing how the level of development in different
> countries is related to quality of life.
>
> (DfES 2000: 8)

> Design and technology: where pupils explore the effects of
> technology on the development of societies and the pupils' own
> lives. By doing this they can develop an understanding of social,
> environmental and sustainable development issues and explore ways
> in which the world can be *improved*. They can learn how the trading
> neighbourhood is the whole planet and that all communities,
> however remote, *are potentially helped by global trade*.
>
> (DfES 2000: 10)

> Design and technology: where pupils learn to design and make
> products and evaluate how a range of different products work. By
> doing this they can ... learn how technology can be used to improve
> the world and contribute to the development of society.
>
> (DfES 2000: 6)

Sustainable development, defined as 'the need to maintain and improve the quality of life now without damaging the planet for future generations' (DfES 2000: 8), is also emphasised and connected to social justice and the 'improved welfare of all people':

> Social justice: understanding the importance of social justice as an
> element in both sustainable development and the improved welfare
> of all people.
>
> (DfES 2000: 8)

On the other hand, global poverty is conceptualised as a 'lack':

> whilst there have been huge improvements that have changed the
> lives of millions of people, one in five of the world's population still
> lives in extreme poverty. They lack access to basic healthcare,

education and clean water, with little opportunity to improve their condition. Moreover, there is increasing acknowledgement of the far-reaching impact of levels of global poverty. Environmental damage, for example, which is exacerbated by poverty, does not stop at national boundaries.

(DfES 2000: 2)

The overemphasis on the benefits of modernity in the document implies that global trade can benefit all communities (and not affect any of them negatively), that there have been changes in the lives of millions of people (only for better), and that environmental damage is exacerbated by poverty (and not by increased consumption). Poverty is seen as a problem of deficit that needs to be dealt with as it has consequences for everyone. However, the connection between the accumulation of wealth and the generation of poverty (e.g. colonial history and unfair trade rules) are foreclosed in the mainstream discourse of the document.

This 'sanctioned ignorance' establishes a patronising attitude towards the South constructed around the notion of global active citizenship. As Spivak (1990) affirms, this can be conceptualised as a 'civilising mission' of the West deriving from the representation of poverty as a lack of resources, services and markets, and of education (as productive of the right subjectivity to participate in the global economy), rather than a lack of control over the production of resources (Spivak 1990; Biccum 2005). The responsibility for poverty is placed upon the poor themselves and the roles of colonialism and unequal power relations and exploitation in the creation of the wealth of the First World are also foreclosed.

This civilising mission of the West to address the poverty-lack by educating the other or dispensing rights remains implicit in the discourse of global citizenship produced in this way. Thus, 'improving the world' becomes the burden of the fittest. North–South power relations and the conditions that created the epistemology and position of privilege of Northern countries are not addressed. This notion reproduces a Eurocentric, logocentric and universalist epistemology, orientalist discourses and colonial power relations, and leaves assumptions of cultural supremacy unchallenged. Within a logocentric epistemology based on the modernisation approach to development, the origins of the wealth of First World countries are detached from exploitation and connected to the discourses of progress of the Enlightenment in terms of human rights, international development, global governance and 'tolerance' in relation to diversity, rationality and the notion of a global community:

> Citizenship: where pupils learn about human rights, the media, the diverse nature of society in the United Kingdom and globally, and the need for mutual respect and understanding. They learn about the role and work of national and international organisations, and the importance of resolving conflict fairly, and develop the skills to discuss and debate topical issues. They learn to consider others' experiences. By doing this they can become informed citizens and understand the world as a global community. They can learn about global governance and address such issues as international development and why it matters. They can develop their interest in topical, global issues and can become willing to take action and actively participate to improve the world.
>
> (DfES 2000: 13)

Active citizenship, then, is turned into providing 'help' in order to 'solve their problems' and 'change the world', as illustrated in one of the case studies in the document:

> GCSE pupils at a girls' school in Birmingham were set the task of producing flash cards to communicate safety issues around the use of electricity in developing countries. Pupils researched ways in which this information could be communicated, taking account of potential problems such as illiteracy. They also considered cultural issues such as the use of the colour red to communicate danger and whether this convention was understood everywhere. Through this project pupils learnt ways in which the quality of life can be improved and to consider the needs and wants of people from different cultures.
>
> (DfES 2000: 10)

From a postcolonial perspective, the assumption behind this initiative is that the 'problem' of developing countries is only based on a 'lack' of attributes that the North possesses (e.g. literacy, education, democracy, scientific knowledge, technology, a more civilised culture, history, universally 'correct' values and so on) and that the North is responsible for the South in the same way that it was believed that the white men had the burden of civilising non-white peoples in colonial times. If, in the period of colonisation, a local (European) set of assumptions of reality and of European supremacy was violently imposed on other people as universal (what Spivak calls an 'epistemic violence'), it can be argued that this could be happening again in the discourses of the global dimension through the concept of 'global citizenship'.

Andrew Dobson (1995) argues that only certain countries have globalising powers; others are globalised. In this sense, the North has a global reach while the South only exists locally. Globalisation is, on this reading, an asymmetrical process in which not only its fruits are divided up unequally, but also in which the very possibility of 'being global' is unbalanced (Dobson 2005: 262). Having the choice to traverse from the local to the global space is the determining factor for whether or not you can be a global citizen. If you are not 'global', the walls built of immigration controls, of residence laws and of 'clean streets' and 'zero tolerance' grow taller (Bauman 1998: 2, cited in Dobson 2005: 263) to try to contain the diffusion of ideas, goods, information and peoples in order to protect specific local spaces from unwanted 'contamination'. Thus, we end up with a one-way transfusion rather than a diffusion (Bauman 1998). As the capacity to act globally is limited, Dobson concludes that those who can and do act globally are in effect often projecting their local (assumptions and desires) as everyone else's global (Dobson 2005: 264). This can be applied to the case study of the school in Birmingham, especially if literacy is conceptualised as the capacity to read how Western knowledge is codified – the problem/lack/deficiency of illiteracy becomes the problem of being 'local' as opposed to 'universal' or global.

Becoming an informed, active, responsible global citizen is the first goal associated with the eight key concepts of the global dimension (DfES 2000: 8) and also surfaces in other parts of the document usually associated with the responsibility to help increase the quality of life (combat poverty) and 'improve the world':

> Key Stages 3 and 4: Pupils develop their understanding of their role as global citizens and extend their knowledge of the wider world. Their understanding of issues such as poverty, social justice and sustainable development increases and they realise the importance of taking action to improve the world for future generations.
>
> (DfES 2000: 10)

Cultural supremacy as discussed by Homi Bhabha (1994) is based on the premise that one group or culture has achieved a better, more developed and universal way of seeing and being. It prompts patronising and paternalistic attitudes towards the South and Southern peoples, as well as a foreclosure – or necessary denial – of the colonial past and of causal responsibility or obligations towards the South. Without this understanding the argument for global citizenship through the development of the global dimension in the school curriculum is left to rest on notions of compassion, charity, 'common humanity' or 'interdependence' that do not necessarily address issues of power, inequalities and injustice. Although compassion and charity are not mentioned in the document, interdependence is one of the eight key concepts and a 'common humanity' features as what lies at the core of diversity (also among the eight key concepts):

> Interdependence: understanding how people, places and environments are all inextricably interrelated and that events have repercussions on a global scale.
>
> (DfES 2000: 9)

> Diversity: understanding and respecting differences and relating these to our common humanity.
>
> (DfES 2000: 9)

they can develop a sense of themselves as members of a world-wide community in which there exists a wide range of cultures and identities but a common humanity.

(DfES 2000: 7)

According to the document, what binds us to people who are different from us is our interdependence and 'common humanity'. If these concepts are combined with other ideas presented so far (i.e. of poverty as a lack and responsibility to help), what emerges is a moral obligation to help/intervene based on a position of privilege.

Dobson argues that acts grounded on this moral basis are easily withdrawn and end up reproducing unequal (paternalistic) power relations and increasing the vulnerability of the recipient (Dobson 2006). For him, justice is a better ground for thinking as it is political and prompts fairer and more equal relations. He proposes that the source of this obligation should be a recognition of complicity or 'causal responsibility' in transnational harm (ibid.).

Dobson states that the globalisation of trade creates ties based on 'chains of cause and effect that prompt obligations of justice, rather than sympathy, pity or beneficence' (2006: 178). He offers the ecological footprint as an illustration of how this operates 'as a network of effects that prompts reflection on the nature of the impacts they comprise' (2006: 177). He also mentions unjust practices imposed by the North as a global institutional order that reproduce poverty and impoverish people (ibid.).

However, these 'alternative' perspectives about the origins of poverty are foreclosed in the document, which makes the position of 'causal responsibility' or 'responsibility towards the other' (as opposed to responsibility for the other), as Spivak (2004) conceptualises it, impossible to envisage.

The conceptualisation of poverty as a lack and seamless narratives of progress, history and development are the norm in the document, but there is one instance where different perspectives are acknowledged and the possibility for multiple causes of poverty (including links with slavery and colonialism) is made explicit:

> pupils can explore some of the causes of world poverty, conflict, immigration, and refugee peoples. They can bring in a global perspective through the study of trade, slavery, empire, colonialism and the commonwealth; they can learn to appreciate the different perspectives on events when seen from different standpoints.
>
> (DfES 2000: 11)

This is the only guideline of the document where a contemplation of different perspectives on history/events is advised, suggesting the existence of multiple histories, discourses and logics. It is the only explicit example of an approach found in this analysis that could potentially challenge assumptions of cultural supremacy. Less explicit and more ambivalent guidelines include the idea of evaluating images of the developing world critically and how representations of less developed countries can shape pupils' own and other views (DfES 2000: 8). Depending on how criticality is conceived, these guidelines could challenge the dominant Eurocentric-universalist perspective presented in the document. However, if the understanding of criticality is also based on universalist and logocentric assumptions, reproducing the idea of possible neutrality, the same strategies could reinforce the dominant assumptions.

Comparison and conclusion

A comparison of DGDSC with a postcolonial perspective shows various points of divergence and is illustrated in Table 4.1. The perception of the problem is the most evident. While DGDSC depicts the problem as the poverty or helplessness of the 'other', resulting from a lack of development, education, resources, skills, knowledge, culture or technology, a postcolonial perspective presents the problem as inequality and injustice originating from complex structures and systems (including systems of belief and psychological internalisations), power relations and attitudes that tend to eliminate difference and maintain exploitation and enforced disempowerment.

Table 4.1 Comparison of developing a global dimension to the school curriculum and a postcolonial perspective

	DGDSC framework	Postcolonial framework
Problem	Poverty, helplessness	Inequality, injustice
Nature of the problem	Lack of 'development', education, resources, skills, culture, technology, etc.	Complex structures, systems, assumptions, power relations and attitudes that create and maintain exploitation and enforced disempowerment and tend to eliminate difference
Justification for positions of privilege (in the North and in the South)	'Development', 'history', education, harder work, better organisation, better use of resources, technology	Benefit from and control over unjust and violent systems and structures
Basis for caring	Common humanity/being good/ sharing and caring	Justice/complicity in harm
	Responsibility *FOR* the other (or to teach the other)	Responsibility *TOWARDS* the other (or to learn with the other) – accountability
Grounds for acting	Humanitarian/moral (based on normative principles for thought and action)	Political/ethical (based on normative principles for relationships)
Understanding of interdependence	We are all equally interconnected, we all want the same thing, we can all do the same thing	Asymmetrical globalisation, unequal power relations, Northern and Southern elites imposing own assumptions as universal
What needs to change	Structures, institutions and individuals that are a barrier to development	Structures, (belief) systems, institutions, assumptions, cultures, individuals, relationships
What for	So that everyone achieves development, harmony, tolerance and equality	So that injustices are addressed, more equal grounds for dialogue are created, and people can have more autonomy to define their own development
Role of 'ordinary' individuals	Some individuals are part of the problem, but ordinary people are part of the solution as they can create pressure to change structures	We are all part of problem and part of the solution
What individuals can do	Support campaigns to change structures, donate time, expertise and resources	Analyse own position/context and participate in changing structures, assumptions, identities, attitudes and power relations in their contexts
Basic principle for change	Universalism (non-negotiable vision of how everyone should live what everyone should want or should be)	Reflexivity, dialogue, contingency and an ethical relation to difference (radical alterity)
Goal of global citizenship education	Empower individuals to act (or become active citizens) according to what has been defined for them as a good life or ideal world	Empower individuals: to reflect critically on the legacies and processes of their cultures and contexts, to imagine different futures and to take responsibility for their decisions and actions
Strategies for the global dimension in education	Raising awareness of global issues and promoting campaigns	Promoting engagement with global issues and perspectives and an ethical relationship to difference, addressing complexity and power relations

	DGDSC framework	Postcolonial framework
Potential benefits of the approach	Greater awareness of some of the problems, support for campaigns, greater motivation to help/do something, feel-good factor	Independent/critical thinking and more informed, responsible and ethical action
Potential problems of the approach	Feeling of self-importance or self-righteousness and/or cultural supremacy, reinforcement of colonial assumptions and relations, reinforcement of privilege, partial alienation, uncritical action	Guilt, internal conflict and paralysis, critical disengagement, feeling of helplessness

Source: Andreotti 2006b.

In relation to the wealth in the North, DGDSC points toward ideas of seamless progress, 'development', participation in a 'universal' history, achievements in science and technology and the realisation of a universal epistemology as justifications for privilege. From a postcolonial or post-development perspective, this privilege comes mostly from Northern control over unjust and violent systems and structures that maintain inequalities.

While DGDSC presents humanitarian and moral grounds for action based on the notion of a 'common humanity' and a sense of responsibility for the other, a postcolonial perspective defends political and ethical grounds for action based on the notion of justice and complicity in harm, or responsibility towards the other.

DGDSC can be interpreted as promoting the need for change in terms of capacity building, and in terms of cultures (belief systems) that are a barrier to development in order to achieve economic growth, equality and tolerance. A postcolonial perspective promotes a change of cultures, relationships and structures so that injustices are addressed, more equal grounds for dialogue are created, and people can have more autonomy to define their own development.

The basic principle for change in DGDSC seems to be universalism – a non-negotiable universalised epistemology that would work for everyone. Thus, the goal of global citizenship education is to empower individuals to act according to what has been defined for them as development, or a good life or ideal world. From a postcolonial perspective the basic principle for change is contingency, dialogue, an ethical relation to difference and reflexivity – a way of engaging critically with the past in order to imagine other possible futures. Therefore, within a postcolonial framework, the goal of 'planetary' citizenship education is to enable individuals to reflect critically on the legacies and processes of their cultures and contexts, to imagine and negotiate 'otherwise', and to take responsibility for their decisions and actions.

Finally, the understanding of interdependence in DGDSC tends to overly emphasise how the North can affect the South in positive ways and how the South can affect the North in negative ways (e.g. by increasing environmental degradation). DGDSC does not address unequal power relations, the history of colonialism or how the North has also affected the South in negative ways.

In conclusion, DGDSC tends to reproduce assumptions of cultural supremacy in implicit and/or explicit ways. Therefore, from a post-colonial perspective, a logical implication is the reinforcement of stereotypes and, potentially, racism in, ironically, precisely the policy initiatives that aim to address these issues. If the aims of the document are to be achieved, a much more reflexive and in-depth discussion of notions of culture, poverty and development should be presented and educational approaches that support the inclusion of different perspectives, critical literacy and independent thinking should be encouraged.

Note
1 The terms 'Global South' or 'North' and 'South' are used as metaphors related to the perception of poverty and privilege in discourses in this area as well as to the divisions in the global distribution of power, labour, mobility and resources.

References

Andreotti, V. (2006a) 'Soft versus critical global citizenship education'. *Development Education Policy and Practice*, 3 (Autumn), 83–98.

—— (2006b) 'A postcolonial reading of contemporary discourses related to the global dimension in Education in England'. Unpublished PhD thesis, University of Nottingham.

Bauman, Z. (1998) *Globalization: The human consequences*. New York: Columbia University Press.

Bhabha, H. (1994) *The Location of Culture*. London: Routledge.

Biccum, A. (2005) 'Development and the "new" imperialism: a reinvention of colonial discourse in DFID promotional literature'. *Third World Quarterly*, 26.6, 1005–20.

Department for Education and Skills (DfES) (2000) *Curriculum and Standards Guidance: Developing a global dimension in the school curriculum*. London: Department for Education and Skills.

Dobson, A. (1995) *Green Political Thought: An introduction*. London: Routledge.

—— (2005) 'Globalisation, cosmopolitanism and the environment'. *International Relations*, 19.3, 259–73.

—— (2006) 'Thick cosmopolitanism'. *Political Studies*, 54.1, 165–84.

Qualifications and Curriculum Authority (QCA) (1999) *Aims and Values of the Curriculum*. London: Department for Education and Skills.

Spivak, G. (1990) *The Post-colonial Critic: Interviews, strategies, dialogues*. New York: Routledge.

—— (2004) 'Righting wrongs'. *South Atlantic Quarterly*, 103.23, 523–81.

Sylvester, C. (1999) 'Development studies and postcolonial studies: disparate tales of the "Third World"'. *Third World Quarterly*, 20.4, 703–21.

5 Global school relationships:[1] school linking and modern challenges

Alison Leonard

Introduction

One of the major areas of expansion in terms of UK government support for development education in the past decade has been through funding schools and non-governmental organisations (NGOs) to promote and engage in linking between schools in the UK and the 'developing world', referred to in much of the literature as 'North–South linking'. As a consequence, linking now has a high profile within both development education and government policy interpretations of how best to deliver understanding and support for development issues within schools.

This chapter aims to address the context for school links and partnerships and the issues and challenges they pose for development education practice. It includes a review of policy changes and recent debates in this area and suggests areas that could be the focus of future research. Specifically the chapter seeks to identify, based on existing literature, how global school relationships are being defined, what the issues are concerning the evaluation of school linking and why South–North linking is a controversial issue. The chapter also discusses what makes an effective global school relationship. Finally, in the light of responses to these questions, it poses challenges to linking practitioners, policy-makers and members of the educational research community on the future direction of school linking, particularly in relation to who defines the nature of the relations and where the power lies.

This chapter is not concerned with other types of school links, such as North–North or South–South school links, nor does it set out to consider fully the motives, purposes and processes of partnerships/links.[2]

How do policy changes impact on the linking process?

Typically global school relationships are 'either about learning (about, from or together) or about development (helping or being helped)' (Najda 2008). Reasons why governments might be interested in the linking process emanate from their domestic and international agenda. The impetus may originate from different government departments, each with differing priorities. In the UK this has ranged from the Department for Education and Skills (DfES), now the Department for Children, Schools and Families (DCSF), largely governed by an educational brief, to the Department for International Development (DFID), with development aims, to HM Treasury. Arguably not all the underlying reasons will sit comfortably with the aims of development education. For schools the major changes which may have affected the process of school linking over the past decade include the introduction of citizenship as part of the national curriculum in England, Wales and Scotland, the DfES's 'Putting the World into World Class Education: An International Strategy for Education, Skills and Children's Services' (2004), their guidance paper, 'Developing the Global Dimension in the School Curriculum' (2005) and the Qualifications and Curriculum Authority (QCA)'s 'The Global Dimension in Action' (2007). Alongside these policies has been the development of initiatives including the Commission for Africa, 'Global Gateway'[3] web portal and Connecting Classrooms venture, DFID and HM Treasury's 'The World Classroom' and the BBC's World Class project,[4] with its emphasis on links in Africa. All these initiatives have influenced and will influence the nature and form of school linking in the UK and the global South. Possibly UK linking with the South is witnessing a divergence between relationships with African schools and the linking process with other Southern participants; perhaps the former is more akin to aims of development and allied NGOs, rather than the aspirations of 'partnership' or development education.

Both citizenship and the global dimension in schools have arguably served as an impetus for the establishment of global school relationships, stimulated by DFID's[5] increased funding for its DFID Global School Partnerships (DGSP) programme.[6] But what do we really know about the impact and effectiveness of such funding? Whose interests will such additional expenditure serve? Do we know what happens to school links when funding stops? Will school linking help to bring about Andreotti's complex, complicated, difficult, worthwhile or potentially 'thin' and superficial understanding?

Leonard (2004a, 2004b, 2005) and Doe (2007) have expressed similar concerns about the drive to meet UK government targets for large-scale participation in linking set for 2010.[7] As a 2007 DFID statement acknowledged: 'a rapid growth in the numbers of UK schools engaged in partnerships with schools in the global South is being promoted by government departments'. What the DfES could not confirm (in 2006, before the formation of the DCSF) is how many of these links are intended to be with Southern schools.

It is dangerous to infer that laudable outcomes will always emerge from the school linking process, the award of project grants, attendance at teachers' continuing professional development training (CPD) or when reciprocal visits are organised.[8] If schools were to adopt Clare Short's 1999 aspiration for every UK school to form a link with a Southern school, then the majority of academics currently contributing to our knowledge base on the process of school linking between Southern and Northern schools urge caution.

Other UK policy changes that are likely to impact on school linking include 'The World Classroom' launched in January 2007: 'Building links between schools across the world, bringing pupils together, sharing experiences and learning will help us tackle the challenge of providing education for all' (Hilary Benn, in DFID 2007: 2), and the Sustainable Schools National Framework, which sets long-term UK government targets for 2020. This comprises 'eight "doorways" through which schools may choose to initiate or extend their sustainable school activity', one of which is the global dimension. The clearly expressed intention for UK schools to act as models of Global Citizenship[9] might be viewed as another imposition of Northern values on Southern partners or neo-colonialism, rather than the reciprocal learning espoused by organisations such as the British Council, the Development Education Association (DEA), United Nations Educational, Scientific and Cultural Organisation (UNESCO) and the United Kingdom One World Linking Association (UKOWLA).

Defining global school relationships?

In the introductory chapter, Bourn outlines the historical context of development education and, as he states, a degree of consensus emerged in the 1990s by NGOs across Europe to summarise the meaning of the term. There has however been less consensus over what is meant by school linking and partnerships, particularly between the economically developing or Southern and economically developed or Northern parts of the world (Andreotti 2006a; Doe 2007; Fricke, 2006; Leonard 2004a, 2004b; Martin 2007; Whitehead 2006).

> A North–South link between schools in the UK and Africa, Asia, Latin America or the Caribbean, is a partnership which is long-term, fully reciprocal, and embedded in the curriculum.
>
> (Central Bureau 1998)[10]

This definition, outlined a decade ago, still underpins the idealised rationale for linking advocated by those organisations supporting the process of school linking, including the British Council, Cambridge Education Foundation, UKOWLA and Voluntary Service Overseas

(VSO);[11] however, things have arguably moved on in the sense that there is now a much wider variety of interpretations of these relationships.

The notion of an association between schools can encompass a wide range of participants and phases in education, from early years (under 5) and primary (first stage compulsory education) through to secondary (aged 11 and over). A school's association with another institution may explore aspects of learning and understanding, both within and beyond the confines of the taught curriculum. This might include developing an awareness of the richness of the other's culture. It might also just be the enjoyment and positive experiences that come from enjoying the opportunity offered by an exchange visit,[12] pupils and teachers talking together and potentially developing personal friendships or sharing in new activities, as evidenced at the Global Gateway website and in a range of personal testimonies and reports compiled by participating schools. And last, but seemingly not least, it might also exemplify a 'charitable' relationship with a school in the North raising funds or other resources for a school link in the South (Fricke 2008).

If school linking and partnerships are seen as covering a wide range of approaches, forms of relationships and contacts between schools, then it is suggested here there is a need to discuss and debate what is meant by these terms.

A key question posed here is the need to clarify what is meant by a partnership and by a link.[13] Should all relationships be long-term, fully reciprocal partnerships embedded in the curriculum, as in the Central Bureau definition? If these characteristics are not demonstrated, do the parties involved not have a link? Whitehead (2006), Burr (2008a) and Scoffham (2008) argue that we should value the outcomes from short-term associations, not just long-term partnerships, and effective links may not be embedded in the curriculum. Short-term projects of mutual interest can serve as a way for schools to engage and longer term relationships may develop as a result of working together on something.

Doe (2007) conducted an audit, on behalf of UNESCO, 'for as many UK international school links as could be found'. He drew on the BBC

World Class website, entries to the *Times Educational Supplement* (TES) Make the Link awards and relationships known to various NGOs, link support agencies and Development Education Centres (DECs). He traced '1,667 overseas partnerships in 1,310 UK schools involving 105 different countries'. What however is uncertain is the status of the associations he identified. The author noted:

> The continuation of all the links found in this search for known links cannot be assumed. In each case a link was counted if there was a public record of its existence and the identity and location of the school could be confirmed.
>
> (Doe 2007: 8)

UKOWLA, in describing when Southern and Northern schools form associations in which pupils, teachers and other members of a school or local community establish a working relationship, refer to the term 'links' and not 'partnerships'. UKOWLA therefore regard it as an important point to make that associations and links cannot automatically be defined as partnerships.

As demonstrated in chapters 1 and 6 in this volume, development education is moving on. It could be claimed that in the last two decades of the twentieth century, development education was perceived as promoting greater awareness and understanding of development issues. For some Northern school linking practitioners this meant gaining insight into the lives of those in the developing world. Today, however, development education generally focuses on exploring the bigger global debates in education: globalisation, interconnectedness, sustainability and interdependence. Can school links facilitate these debates?

This therefore poses the need to clarify our terminology, since within the classifications lurk dilemmas for people engaged in development education and for practitioners engaged in school linking. For example: to what extent should the debates on school linking be framed within and complement current debates in development education (raised in chapters 2, 4 and 6 in this volume) in relation to questions of power, social change and learning processes?

It is suggested here that perhaps the most important of these debates in terms of development education and school linking is the issue of power relationships. Is it a backward step to claim that when a Southern school embraces the opportunities offered by an association with a Northern one, they enjoy a partnership? Partners enjoy joint shares in a relationship, jointly take decisions and complement one another. It can be argued that 'A *partner* participates in a relationship in which each member has equal status'.[14] If we apply the term partner imprecisely to schools whose associations are merely links are we glossing over the uncomfortable evidence that schools may be far from equal? This potential power imbalance is exemplified in a quotation referred to by advocates, practitioners and researchers: 'First you came to us as missionaries, then you came to us as colonisers, now you come to us as linkers' (Southern MUNDI conference participant in 2002).

Perhaps we could view the process of school linking as a continuum, encompassing links and a variety of different types of partnership, as shown in a simplified model in Figure 5.1. Taking the 'global dimension' into the difficult debates that Bourn (see Chapter 1) has challenged development educators to explore, school relationships wherever they are on a 'Linking–partnership' continuum must respond to notions of educational change and tackle controversial, contentious issues. As Disney (2004), Martin (2006) and Andreotti (2006b, 2007) have commented, school linking could, without due care by practitioners 'come dangerously near to epitomising a new form of colonialism' (Disney 2004: 146).

A better term for many links between Southern schools and their Northern counterparts would be 'global school relationships'; because if the term 'partnership' is used too loosely it devalues those school associations that are genuine 'partnerships'. The plea by both Bourn (Chapter 1) and Hicks (2005) for development educators to apply greater conceptual clarity and rigour must be evident in our application of terminology. If we are describing a school relationship in which we acknowledge that parties do not enjoy equality and that common goals are not necessarily intrinsic to the association, but that valuable

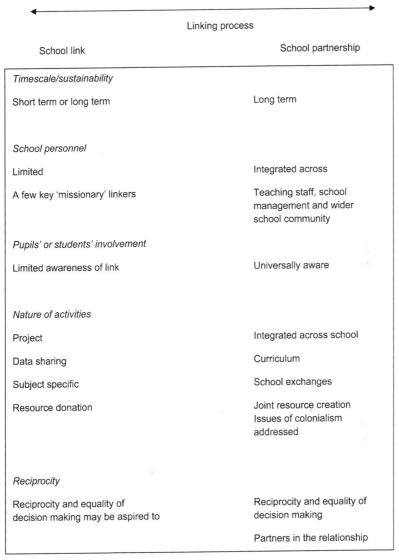

Figure 5.1 A simplified school linking–partnership continuum

Note: Exemplar indicator linking-process characteristics are shown in italics.

educational opportunities can develop, is it a partnership? Pupils, teachers and members of the wider school community could still explore global concepts such as interdependence, citizenship and stewardship, diversity, sustainable development, social justice, values and perceptions and human rights.[15] It could therefore be posed, why claim that a 'partnership' exists? Why not apply the term 'school link' and acknowledge that until the financial element of the relationship and the role of linked schools in decision making is one of equality it is unhelpful, inappropriate and misleading to claim they enjoy a partnership?

It is therefore suggested that there is a need to establish the agreed purposes and criteria for a linking process and to identify distinctions between types of linking relationships. There is also a need to clarify whose values are being used in the process and evaluation of a linking programme. It may be helpful to refer to a continuum of linking relationships; some possible indicator characteristics to facilitate the placing of global schools' relationships on such a continuum are suggested in Figure 5.1, although these are not intended by this author to be exclusive.

Should we take greater care in our application of terminology, acknowledging that a continuum of global school relationships exists, as postulated in Figure 5.1?[16] Schools' entry points onto such a continuum may differ; schools may move along the continuum, towards the Central Bureau's and subsequently LSO's (2000) and DFID's 'aspirational' outcomes of mutuality, reciprocity, equality of decision making, durability, embedding in school curricula and concepts such as friendship or the DGSP 'idealised view of partnership' evolution (2007: 11). Such outcomes may not or perhaps cannot necessarily exist when a linking process starts; time and effort for teachers' CPD, developing sensitivity and sustaining the relationship cannot be presumed at the outset. Some participants may embark on a fixed-term initiative with the understanding that you may or may not want to try to turn the relationship into a longer term link; others may not progress towards partnership, but remain as links (Burr 2008a). Scoffham asks if we should recognise that the process: 'doesn't need to involve equal exchange but can be asymmetrical. Northern and Southern needs are markedly different. It is perfectly valid for both partners to bring different things to the relationship' (2008).

Evaluating the school linking process

> How do we avoid, what we call in the trade, just an enthusiastic 'victory narrative' without a robust evidence base?
>
> (Gaine 2006: 11)

> I have doubts about the enterprise ... I think School Linking has dangers. It runs the risk of being superficial, or patronising, or short-lived, or uncritically benevolent.... It runs the risk of reinforcing things as they are.
>
> (Gaine 2006: 12)

The debates around terminology concerning relationships and partnerships pose the question of the purpose, value and impact of the link. For example, how does linking impact on pupils' learning? What timescale should be used to judge the impacts of school links? Each of these questions will now be considered in regard to reviews of current debates and research on these questions.

Outcomes for pupils' learning

Advocates of development education and school linking include prominent British and Irish political figures (Benn 2007;[17] Brown;[18] Kitt;[19] Knowles 2000; Leftwich 2006a, 2006b; Lenihan 2006;[20] Short 1999). They celebrate the benefits for participating Northern pupils. There is relatively little research literature focused on empirical analysis (Burr 2003; Irish Aid 2006), including those for Southern participants in the process. Leonard's (2004a, 2004b, 2005) research in British schools revealed that some statistically significant differences in pupil learning about development issues did occur when schools formed educational alliances. The quality of teaching and learning in the 'Global Dimension' was affected positively by the presence of a school link. The differences between the pupils' responses in the linked and non-linked school samples were statistically significant in response to only five of the ten questions analysed. These were: the associations brought to mind by 'developing or third world', views that 'There is more that unites us than divides us from people in poorer countries', 'Third world countries often bring poverty, famine and crises on themselves' and 'I would be interested in watching more television that shows everyday life, history, culture and people in developing countries' and pupils' responses to 'the most positive thing that you can do to help build a global community.' However, the author noted that proponents of a linking process may be disappointed by some learning outcomes, such as the persistence of pupils' perceived 'development stereotypes'; while Burr (2008a) cautions, 'we all know examples of where links have been detrimental to Global Dimension understanding'.

> In December 2004 a school in The Gambia received a 1992 Dell computer, a 1988 RM Nimbus machine and a 1981 BBC microcomputer. This out of date equipment did not even have any accompanying software, discs or instructions. There had been a grand ceremony to receive this gift from a UK school. Arriving in January 2005 I had to tell them how useless this equipment was, but although clearly disappointed they did not note this in the questionnaire on linking they were completing, until assured that the source of information would remain anonymous.
>
> (Burr 2008b: 3)

Leonard's analysis was restricted to pupils studying Geography at key stage 3 (aged 11–14) and therefore its claimed impacts were narrowly defined. Williams (2006a) queried: 'Was it the links that made the difference or were these linked schools predisposed to a greater commitment in this area anyway?' Anecdotal evidence has indicated that sometimes negative consequences (Martin 2005) or inaccurate stereotypes can even become further ingrained as a result of linking, while school exchange visits can be particularly problematic. How do you compare twenty students for example going from the UK with the much smaller numbers coming here, often only a couple? How should we respond to Southern students reportedly dropping out of school because they will never have what they have seen in the West (Burr 2007a, 2008a)?

There also remains a need to investigate further the nature of both positive and negative impacts of the linking process, not only on the quality of pupil learning but on wider aspects, including those on teachers' CPD (Martin 2007) and the transfer of understanding gained to the wider community in which linked schools sit, at both ends of a North–South link, as advocated by Burr (2003, 2006):

> Linking provides a unique opportunity for young people to engage with, and learn from, others. It can facilitate direct involvement in an issue, such as raising awareness on the plight of the Western Saharans in refugee camps. It can help to broaden horizons, stimulate involvement and most importantly provide young people with a voice and make them aware that they, themselves, can effect change. The benefits of linking are often clear for schools in the 'North', but for Southern partners the benefits are not so clear and each link needs to be considered carefully.

This chapter however cannot explore this issue in depth; we need to know why this happens and how this can be overcome (Andreotti *et al.* 2007). Part of linking preparation must be in educating each participant's expectations of the other.

What is clear from reviewing the research literature in this area is that there is still very little empirical data to make any substantive observations on the impact of linking on pupils' learning. This clearly has to be addressed if this area of educational practice continues to receive considerable resources and policy support.

Assessing the lasting impact of the linking process

The prerequisite for an evidence base to assess the impact of school linking has been forcefully advocated by several commentators (Bond

1996; Burr 2003, 2007b, 2008b; Doe 2007; Egan 2006; Fricke 2006; Gaine 2006; Heyes 2006; Leonard 2004, 2005; Martin 2006; Najda 2008; Schirher 2006; Williams 2006a, 2006b). There is need for this evidence not only to underpin future policies, but also to promote best practice advice and arguably extend such initiatives beyond contemporary participants.

Particularly in assessing the impact (i.e. the longer lasting, sustained consequences of a school link or partnership), a need of future research is to monitor a range of participants over a longer timescale than has been attempted so far: beyond pupils and teaching staff currently in linked schools. Should we know, for example, how participation in school exchanges and study visits subsequently has an impact on pupils, teachers and other participants?[21] Such long-term follow-up of linking participants is probably more difficult to conduct than existing evaluations, yet to assess the effectiveness of a linking process it should not be ignored. If we are to understand how the link impacts on participants over time is there also a need to assess the efficacy of different elements and manifestations of the linking process?

The majority of the existing evidence base is of short-term impacts of the linking process, often conducted by participants for those funding linking initiatives, such as the British Council and the UK's DGSP programme.[22] Does such evaluation pose difficult, controversial, contentious questions about the linking process? If negative responses could be seen to threaten future participation in an alliance that brings educational advantages and possibly financial benefits, will participants' positive criticisms be recorded officially, or might they remain unvoiced, for fear of threatening the linking process (Andreotti 2007)? Such a potential compromise of the evaluative process is probably most likely to apply at the Southern end of a schools' global link, since the fundholder, certainly for most links supported by DGSP, is generally the Northern partner.[23] How does this encourage reciprocity in a linking relationship? Is there an inherent risk that Southern participants may feel compelled to minimise formative criticism or assessment, demonstrating Disney's neo-colonialism referred to earlier? Could this hinder a link's progress towards equality in decision making and movement along a linking–partnership continuum towards partnership?

It will be illuminating to observe the evolution of new links established between Irish schools and their Southern partners, since the publication of Irish Aid's linking review (O' Keeffe 2006). Lacking from the linking process for existing Irish/Southern links are the vestiges of economic colonialism and paternalism that may impact British/Southern links or those between other Northern participants with links in their former colonial territories. However, since historically many Irish/Southern links have been associated with a 'missionary background' the charitable element of such links may also complicate such relationships, frustrating the development of the equality and reciprocity indicators which characterise the partnership end of the continuum shown in Figure 5.1. Might such links demonstrate the vestiges of 'charitable colonialism' rather than economic colonialism, paternalism or neo-colonialism[24] that can complicate other North/South links?

A large-scale two-year evaluation of school partnerships for the UK government[25] was initiated in Autumn 2006. Amongst its remit are intended outcomes such as a mini report on 'the state of the field', and a full report on 'how school partnerships influence schools'. It remains to be seen whether this study will create the 'robust evidence base' Gaine and others seek; will those interviewed feel able to feel comfortable in expressing their views? Burr (2008b) for example noted: 'it can be seen as churlish to find fault with something so seemingly "beneficial" as people forming links'. There are always the dangers of 'short-termism' and 'victory narratives' from such evaluations in the field of development education. However as the evaluation is being led by a well-respected university with considerable expertise in research, there is the hope that for the first time evidence will emerge that begins to address some of the questions posed in this chapter.

To pursue a large-scale longitudinal study of the school linking process an opportunity potentially exists to revisit participants of the 516 global school links established in the millennium under the auspices of the 'On the Line' project (Atchison 2001; Leonard 2004a, 2004b; Moore 1999; Temple 2006b). Since these links were all set up within a restricted time period they could provide the chance for a longitudinal study as advocated above.

South–North linking as a controversial issue

South–North school relationships have been dogged by a number of controversies and they mirror wider debates within development education related to issues of power, whose voices are being promoted, whose and what values underpin the practice and what is the relationship between learning and action. The key issues debated here in this chapter are values, action, fund-raising, equality and understanding. In the context of the linking process the key questions could be summarised: Whose values matter in evaluation? Is 'active participation' a desirable outcome of the linking process? Are equality and reciprocity of benefits possible, desirable or essential? Can global school relationships result in 'thin', superficial understanding? For example when using learning opportunities from the linking process to compare and contrast wealth and poverty across the global divide, do pupils investigate the underlying reasons for such inequalities in wealth? Do learners explore the distinction between poverty and quality of life? Do they discuss our attitudes towards charity and aid and the patronage or disempowerment that this involves? Do teachers examine their own ideas about themselves and their identity? (Scoffham 2007, 2008). Burr observed teachers rarely 'look into the causes of poverty and injustice seeing the area as too political and controversial' (2000b).

Whose values matter?

How to assess participation in linking relationships can be viewed as a values-laden conundrum; whose values or perceptions matter? Educators conducting action research and reflective classroom teachers refine their planning in the light of observed, sometimes unintended learning outcomes; this is promoted as good practice. If school linking participants similarly refine projects, personnel or practices, straying from planned, agreed criteria, does that diminish the linking process, when an evaluation is conducted? Are the views of all pupils and others in a link canvassed, or is the evaluation restricted to teachers or even linking coordinators? Are long-term influences considered at all?

'Active participation' in linking

The dilemma of participants taking positive action, especially fund-raising activities, is often central to school linking relationships (Andreotti 2006b; Burr 2007a, 2007b, 2008a, 2008b; Disney 2003; Doe 2007; Fricke 2006; Leftwich 2006a, 2006b; Martin 2006; Osler 1994; Williams 2006a, 2006b). This educational drive for pupils to 'play an active role as future citizens and members of society' is identified by Martin as central to 'why there is controversy over school linking'. Are such effects potentially reinforcing paternalism? Should stringent constraints on fund-raising be imposed on all school links? Would some participants still engage in the linking process at all? If a link is effective at improving resources in schools and education systems is that a desirable outcome? Or by including fund-raising within a relationship, even if it is a follow-up outcome, is this not as Andreotti, Disney, Egan, Martin and Najda suggest, merely reproducing dependency relationships?

Equality and reciprocity (of benefits)

The question of equality and reciprocity is therefore a key issue within school links. Leftwich, a UK linking coordinator, has completed two unpublished Masters assignments evaluating the impact of her school link.[26] She explored its impacts on students and how outcomes of CPD arising from the link contribute to personal, departmental and school developments. In both she raised concerns and issues requiring further analysis and academic study. In response to a question about her major concern she responded:

> I suppose the same that always comes up – equality whilst remaining ever aware of the cultural differences and emphases. All grants are led by the Northern partner and it can be a very stressful experience when the Southern partner doesn't understand why things have to be done in such a way – because the grants are all Northern created and written as well.
>
> (Leftwich 2006)[27]

Doe has identified that similar concerns are shared by Southern participants and educationalists:

> The success of such links, however, depends on the perception of mutual benefit. At the Cape Town ministers' conference and the Commonwealth Consortium for Education conference on school linking which preceded it, suspicion was expressed by some that the expansion of UK school partnerships was intended to enrich the UK curriculum rather than benefit schools in partner countries.
>
> (Doe 2007: 5)

This is particularly so when schools form ad hoc links, through measures such as DFID's Global Gateway,[28] which was: 'Seen by some as resulting in arrangements between partners which may not be equal and which did not engage with developing countries' own school improvement agendas' (Doe 2007: 5). He referred specifically to South African assessments of the effectiveness of the linking process, one even questioning 'if there was any real benefit from North–South partnerships – particularly those based on the idea of exporting first-world technical expertise to the expertise-poor',[29] while another, Naledi Pandor, South Africa's Education Minister, regretted that political rhetoric was not matched by current linking practices:

> Gordon Brown signalled an important shift in thinking away from *ad hoc* links towards a focus on the benefits of partnerships for schools and education systems in the South. Unfortunately most funding

agencies and policy-makers in the North have not shifted with him and are still mainly concerned about the advantage for children of the North.

(Doe 2007: 5)

Can global school relationships result in 'thin', superficial understanding?

Williams's (2006a, 2006b) assessment of the impact of linking activities,[30] as true of most current literature, encapsulated by Pandor's criticism, examined linking outcomes for Northern students. He found that linking events didn't necessarily generate a depth of involvement, the 'thin' understanding of development issues, to which Bourn (2006a) has alluded. Andreotti (2006b, 2008) argues that if we fail to examine the complex 'web of cultural and material local/global processes and contexts' we may end up promoting a 'civilizing mission', reproducing power relations similar to those in colonial times. She advocates that we should move towards an approach based on critical literacy and independent thinking (Lissner 1977), which crystallised into the Open Spaces for Dialogue and Enquiry (OSDE)[31] initiative. Is this a methodology for the introduction of global issues and perspectives in education or potentially a pedagogy for development education, including school linking (Alexander 2004)? Andreotti's aspiration to facilitate a learning environment in which the complicated, challenging, difficult concepts can be grappled with to greatest effect must be adequately resourced, however: 'The production of worthwhile material demands time, resources and cooperation' (Osler 1994).

Writing in the context of projects that could help to break down perceptions of the 'Third World or South as a monolithic bloc', Osler raised eight questions before such projects should begin, three directly related to funding issues. Like Andreotti et al. (2008), Olser also effectively encapsulated a challenge for teachers as educators, which OSDE's methodology relies upon, claiming educators need to 'recognize that the deficiencies of our own education' may compromise efforts to become effective development educators, warning further of the dangers if teachers fail to address questions of development at an adult level.

Williams's students demonstrated an interest in international development issues; however, with high profile international campaigns such as Make Poverty History and Live8 fresh in pupils' recent experience it was difficult to isolate the influence of the linking process. He questioned, for example, what students actually understood the diverse Make Poverty History campaign to be: 'Were the majority taking a simplistic view such as "helping poor children in Africa"?' (2006a: 7).

Evaluating the effectiveness of the linking process in changing attitudes and promoting pupil action, he concluded: 'we can say that there was an impact on the older students', but there remains an inherent difficulty in identifying exactly what had caused the change in attitude which his students reported. It would appear that this dilemma might compromise other researchers' efforts to isolate and distinguish the impact of the linking process from pre-existing dispositions, however: 'Xamul aay na, laajtewul a ko raw: Not to know is bad, not to wish to know is worse' (Commission for Africa 2005: 2).

What makes an effective global school relationship?

> A school link isn't essential to developing your pupils as global
> citizens; it's only one of a whole range of ways you can do this.
> School linking shouldn't be developed simply to tick the box marked
> 'global citizenship'.
>
> (Temple 2006a: 14)

To provide authoritative advice on good practice we must isolate the characteristics which promote linking effectiveness, potentially stimulating more relationships to move along the linking–partnership continuum, even if such analysis reveals surprises, questions current orthodoxy, funding and policy, or may radically challenge the location of global school links.[32] 'North/South' linking has dominated the pattern, especially in the UK's experience; South/South (Doe 2007) North/North and urban/rural models (Heyes 2006; Komeja 2006) deserve evaluation; the traditional bilateral, school-to-school nature of the linking process may prove outmoded models in future (Egan 2006; Whitehead 2006).

Can development and development education goals coexist in the linking process? A key feature of modern school linking is the complex array of supporting agencies engaged in providing advice and support to schools which by their very nature pose questions about motivations behind the promotion of linking, from funding to education for social change to supporting primarily agendas within Southern countries. There is a need to consider the relationships and whether they can complement each other or whether in reality the needs of educational projects in the South cannot be seen alongside agendas for raising awareness in the North. This relates to the issue posed: Should we 'distinguish between programmes that are based on promoting development education and a global dimension, and those with other aims?' (Egan 2007).

Funding for ICT provision

Should 'charity' and 'aid' be discouraged; do they represent linking paternalism? Funding for information and communication technology (ICT) provision in a Southern school by its linked Northern school may represent a laudable aspect of a global school relationship, but it could equally be viewed as 'technological paternalism' or, as Pandor (Doe 2007: 5) hinted, mainly for the advantage of Northern pupils. How many outdated, 'cast-off', unused personal computers (PCs), for example, lie languishing in Southern schools, shipped and donated by magnanimous yet possibly unthinking Northern partners (Burr 2007a, 2007b)?[33] Did donors fully research the implications before generously donating their old equipment; did they ask if it was needed or did they ask what was needed? Would a City Academy in London, Manchester or Birmingham happily receive 'charitable' donations of worn-out physical education equipment from a commercial sports equipment sponsor?

The location of Southern participants

A further controversial aspect of global school relationships is where they are located in the South. Researchers have questioned whether a desire for Northern participants to communicate with the Southern end of a link using ICT may skew the location of Southern participants to locations in urban areas, which enjoy such facilities, possibly further disadvantaging educational provision in rural areas (Cutler 2005; Petersen 2005). Petersen was not constrained by the current apparent Western 'anti-assistance' rhetoric, arguing that wider participation and benefit from the observed improvements in teaching and enthusiasm and participation from pupils could result. Is it a Northern imposed value to restrict 'assistance' and hence another example of paternalism?

Educational reasons for linking

Martin (2007) warns against Temple's inferred linking as a 'panacea' for global citizenship, emphasising that difficult, controversial dilemmas lack easy answers. Like Fricke (2006) she cautions against school links which 'quickly become educationally meaningless', but concludes in a more positive light that the process 'can be challenging in an exciting and enjoyable way for all involved' acknowledging that her own partic- ipation in study visits to Gambia have contributed significantly to her thinking on the topic. She reviews how different ideologies and values affect school linking, suggesting that the driving forces for the process provide their own cultural, political, ideological and educational contexts and 'this is where some of the tensions begin'. She urges clarity in the educational reasons for linking, claiming teachers should engage with and question their own assumptions and values about develop- ment issues, echoing other researchers' advice that learning takes time and is 'profoundly affected by different cultural expectations'. She does, however, cite William Scott's work on sustainable developments, indicating that when participants have incompatible value-sets learning can be particularly useful if teachers and pupils then challenge their prejudices and reassess their views, but cautions that intercultural contact does not necessarily lead to this type of learning.

Emerging global school relationships

Finally, should the traditional bilateral model of linking be rethought? Multi-agency,[34] multi-participant[35] and cross-phase links in education – combining primary and secondary schools and institutions of higher education (HE) or initial teacher education (ITE) – may prove more effective relationships in some instances than the simple school-to-school links which have dominated the last thirty years of global school relationships (Cogan 2003 and Stevens 2003, both cited in Leonard 2004a; Newell-Jones 2005; Whitehead 2006). A financial commitment, or charge, incurred by Northern participants to ensure the maintenance of such links could prove useful in advancing long-term developments in a linking relationship, or would this be regarded as:

> The type of regressive model that perpetuates unequal and neo-colonial relationships. This model inevitably accentuates the problem of the Southern school being the grateful and uncritical recipient of a Northern benefactor, and takes the focus away from learning and education and back towards charity and aid.
>
> (Egan 2007)

There is an urgent need to assess which types of global school relationships are most effective in which circumstance, whilst remembering that impacts in the wider local community too should be considered during the evaluative process. When can short-term links achieve valuable learning or when can they be potentially damaging? When might a long-term partnership be nearing its conclusion? Are clusters of schools linked together a better model than a partnership of only two?

Conclusion

Five modern challenges have been identified for the future direction of school linking:

1 *A need to clarify terminology*
Practitioners, supporters, policy-makers and researchers should apply care in how they define school associations. In defining terminology for the process of school linking a continuum of relationships is proposed: some participants may embark on a link, which can develop into a partnership, but even then the association may have junior and senior, rather than equal, partners.

2 *A continuing requirement for evaluation of the linking process across a range of formats and locations*
There remains a need for the educational research community to create an evidence base on the effectiveness of a variety of linking relation-ships; to investigate further the nature of linking impacts, not only on the quality of pupil learning but on wider aspects, including those of teachers' CPD and the reach of links into the wider community. Traditional bilateral, school-to-school, pupil-to-pupil linking may prove outmoded models in future as the linking process diversifies into new forms. If differences are emerging between the nature of the linking process with Africa and other developing countries perhaps future analysis may need to distinguish between linking relationships in different parts of the world, rather than regarding global school rela-tionships as a monolithic bloc.

3 *Opportunities to undertake longitudinal studies*
To pursue a large-scale longitudinal study of the school linking process at least three opportunities exist for academic researchers to revisit linking participants: first, to study those links established under the auspices of the On the Line project (Atchison 2001; Leonard 2004a, 2004b; Moore 1999; Temple 2006b); second, to study Northern Irish

schools embarking on the linking process in response to the compulsory introduction of citizenship at key stage 3. Third, it would be interesting to evaluate the evolution of new links between Irish schools and their Southern partners. Since historically many Irish/Southern links have been associated with a 'missionary background', a 'charitable colonialism' element may impact on these links (O' Keeffe 2006).

4 *The identification of characteristics promoting effective linking*

To provide authoritative advice on good practice researchers must continue to isolate the characteristics that promote successful global school relationships, even if such analysis reveals surprises, questions current orthodoxy, funding and policy, or may radically challenge the location and nature of school links. We need to know: how is mutuality manifest in the linking process? What gains are there for Southern schools and their educational improvement agenda? Is there an effectual voice for the South? What are the impacts from teachers' CPD, positive and negative? There is an urgent need to assess which types of global school relationships are most effective, whilst remembering that impacts in the wider local community too should be considered during the evaluative process. Different aspects of the linking process should be isolated, to distinguish how global school relationships support learners, teachers and other participants. The role of links in helping to raise educational attainment is an aspect of the school linking process which should be analysed at both ends, over a longer timescale than has presently been attempted.

5 *The adoption of a preferred methodology or pedagogy*

In the political context, a brief review of the impacts of UK political initiatives suggests that Northern schools may embark on school links in response to government imposed criteria. The creation of links resulting from such large-scale initiatives is questionable in terms of the profundity of understanding which emanates, whilst some Southern educationalists even doubt that mutual benefits accrue. Does or should UK and other Northern policy serve the interests of Southern schools? How far do the UK's 2007 World Classroom initiative and UNESCO's Education for All campaign complement one another? Or can well-intentioned, yet irresponsible 'tokenism' flourish as school linking, or even 'partnerships'? Finally, should linking proponents promote a methodology such as OSDE, fostering depth of under-standing, addressing a combination of the aims of development and development education?

Notes

Thanks go to a veritable host of people interested in global school relationships, who have kindly commented on earlier versions of this chapter: Andy Egan, Ruth Najda and colleagues at the British Council, for DGSP; Vanessa Andreotti, Ali Brownlie Bojang, Anna Disney, Margaret Burr, Harm-Jan Fricke, Gavin Griffiths, Fran Martin, Hugh Morrison, Stephen Scoffham and especially Doug Bourn.

1 The term 'global school' relationships used means links involving schools across the globe.
2 < http://www.britishcouncil.org/globalschools-what-is-dfid-global-school-partnerships.htm> (30 January 2008).
3 This is criticised later in this chapter by Southern educationalists. An apparent incongruity can be observed in published materials on this British Council-managed and DCSF-funded web portal of a case study between Northern schools' fund-raising activities or aid and DfID Global Schools Partnerships (DGSP)'s refusal of grant funding applications where 'there is evidence of a one-sided or charitable relationship'. For example, of six case studies on the web portal, the one featuring a South–North Link, a UK primary school deputy head teacher's report on a School Linking visit, cites four out of ten ways forward in the linking process which directly refer to such initiatives <www.globalgateway.org.uk/default.aspx?page=3315> (6 January 2008).
4 'The intention of the BBC World Class project is to raise awareness of the bene-fits of international school linking with our audience and support linking through our online service' <www.bbc.co.uk/worldclass> (January 2008).
5 'Following more than a doubling of present funding for DFID Global School Partnerships, the programme is announcing a significant increase in the number of grants available for partnerships between UK schools and schools in Africa, Asia, Latin America and the Caribbean' (DfID, London, 28 June 2006).
6 This is a consortium of the British Council, Cambridge Education Foundation, United Kingdom One World Linking Association (UKOWLA) and Voluntary Service Overseas (VSO).

7 Doe inferred that to accommodate the required number of 20,000 new links the majority, 17,000, would have to be in primary schools; can such young pupils achieve a deep understanding of the complexity of global interdependence or is tokenism inevitable, based on pupils' intellectual development at this stage?

8 Some Southern schools are no longer engaging as hosts in exchanges since they question the reciprocity and Southern benefits of this aspect of the linking process.

9 'By 2020 the Government would like all schools to be models of good global citizenship, enriching their educational mission with activities that improve the lives of people living in other parts of the world.'

10 Central Bureau (1998) *School Partnerships with the South. A handbook for UK schools linking with Africa, Asia, Latin America and the Caribbean.* London: Central Bureau.

11 As mentioned earlier, these four agencies currently manage the UK DGSP programme.

12 Although such a 'tourist gaze' is problematic too (Andreotti 2008; Burr 2008a).

13 <www.ukowla.org.uk/main/toolkit.asp> (26 January 2008; Leaflet 3: Partnership.

14 < http://www.thefreedictionary.com/partner>

15 Identified as strands of the 'Global Dimension' in British schools since March 2005.

16 Developments in a linking process may not be unidirectional and participants in schools may not all share the same values. Advice to UK participants exists on how to discontinue such relationships, referred to as an 'Exit Strategy' in current guidance from the DGSP programme (2007: 42).

17 UK Secretary of State for International Development, when quoted.

18 Quoted in British Council (2006). UK Chancellor of the Exchequer at the time and now UK Prime Minister.

19 Quoted in Irish Aid (2007).

20 Quoted in Irish Aid (2006). Irish Minister of State responsible for Irish aid and human rights.

21 These may include members of an extended school community, such as parents, ex-pupils on gap-year work placements and governors or staff members of institutions of higher and further education.

22 Overseen for DfID by the British Council.

23 Of Doe's 1,667 overseas partnerships, mentioned previously, 1,331 were DGSP supported. 'Southern schools are increasingly taking the lead in grant funding applications to DGSP, and grants are not issued to schools where there is evidence of a one-sided or charitable relationship' (Egan 2007).

24 Neo-colonialism is defined here as 'The use of economic, political, cultural, or other pressures to control or influence another country; *especially* the retention of

such influence over a developing country by a former colonial power' (*Oxford English Dictionary*, online version 2007).
25 Described by its lead researcher, Edge (2006) as 'A Study of the Impact of North South School Partnerships on UK, African and Asian Schools' and funded for the first year by DfID, with an advisory group of several high-profile interested UK organisations.
26 Polesworth High School is linked with Pampawie in Ghana; this was instrumental in Polesworth being awarded International Secondary School of the Year in the TES/HSBC Make the Link awards 2006 (GSP (2006) News Issue 3).
27 Personal communication.
28 It is not possible accurately to identify how many such links have been established.
29 Some definitions of the global economic divide substitute 'IT resource rich' and 'IT resource poor' to replace terms such as North, More Economically Developed Country (MEDC) or Economically More Developed Country (EMDC) and South, Less Economically Developed Country (LEDC) or Economically Less Developed Country (ELDC).
30 Two schools were linked following Williams's participation in a Link Community Development (LCD) global teacher placement in 2001. LCD links around 800 schools with development projects in rural Ghana, South Africa, Uganda and Malawi involving 1,500 schools. <http://www.lcd.org.uk/uk/lsp/about.html> (6 January, 2008). Oldfield School in Bath is linked with Mtengwane Senior Secondary School, situated in the Eastern Cape, South Africa. Williams's research questions included: Are UK students aware of the link? To what extent do they understand the physical, cultural and economic conditions in which their fellow learners live and, when faced with an opportunity to make a difference, are they more likely to take action?
31 <www.osdemethodology.org.uk>
32 < www.ukowla.org.uk/main/toolkit.asp>
33 When linked with a Ghanaian school as part of the On the Line project, for example, it was an exciting prospect for my Year 6 pupils in London to communicate electronically with our Southern partners in Accra; however the fund-raising carried out to facilitate this educational outcome was used to purchase new equipment in Ghana, which could be affordably serviced locally. In 2005 and 2006, on exchange visits to a rural Ghanaian senior secondary school linked with a UK secondary school electrical equipment donated several years earlier was either redundant or locked away in an underused ICT facility, its use further compromised by intermittent electricity supplies and the high cost or unavailability of replacement parts and problems in local servicing.
34 Such as NGOs, DECs and other support agency involvement. DGSP is an example of a multi-agency.

35 The British Council's Connecting Classrooms programme, for example, involves a three-way linking process between schools. Each consists of three clusters of three schools from the UK and two sub-Saharan African countries. For successful applicants: 'Each partnership of nine schools is entitled to £15,000 per year to fund project costs including travel' <http://www.britishcouncil.org/learning-connecting-classrooms.htm> (6 January 2008).

Bibliography

Adran Hyfforddiant ac Addysg/ Department for Training and Education ACCAC (2005) 'Secondary school map for curriculum planners - education for sustainable development and global citizenship'. National Assembly for Wales Circular No: 11/2005.

Alexander, T. (2004) 'Learning, the web and global citizenship'. *Development Education Journal*, 11.3 ICT in Global Learning Education.

Andreotti, V. (2006a) 'Soft versus critical global citizenship education'. *Policy and Practice*, 3, Autumn, Centre for Global Education, Belfast.

—— (2006b) Personal communication.

—— (2007) Personal communication.

—— (2008) Personal communication.

Andreotti, V., Burr, M. and Mario de Souza, L. (2007) 'The southern voice in linking: thinking about North/South linking'. PowerPoint presentation.

Atchison, H. (2001) 'Did we make a difference?' *Development Education Journal*, 7.3.

Athill, C. (2005) 'Is e-learning ethical?' *Development Education Journal*, 11.3 ICT in Global Learning Education.

Bailey, H. (2005) Communication during debate: the domestic politics of international aid. Global Development Forum 7, London, 16 March.

Benn, H. (2006) 'Development Beyond Aid'. Fifth White Paper Speech, Chatham House/BOND, 23 February. <http://www.dfid.gov.uk/news/files/Speeches/wp2006-speeches/beyond-aid230206.asp>

—— (2007) 'Developing global partnerships in education: the world classroom'. Press release, 4 January. <http://www.dfid.gov.uk/news/files/pressreleases/world-classroom.asp>

Bibby, A., DEA and Commission for Africa Secretariat (2005) *Our Common Interest. What does the Commission for Africa report say?* Glasgow: DFID.

Bond, B. (1996) *North South Linking Who benefits?* Marlborough: UKOWLA.

Bourn, D (2006a) *Development Education: From practice to a theory of learning.* London: Institute of Education.

—— (2006b) Personal communication.

Brake, T. (2005) Communication during debate: the domestic politics of international aid. Global Development Forum 7, London, 16 March.

British Council (2006) *Global Schools Partnership Advice.* London: British Council. <www.britishcouncil.org/globalschools-partnership-advice-agreement.htm>

Brough, D.R and Cort, G. (1997) The Power Maths Project 'Meeting the challenge of the new technologies'. Paper presented at the PEG Conference, Sozopol, Bulgaria. powermaths@aol.com

Burr, M. (2003) Personal communication – copy of article produced for the British Council.

—— (2006) Personal communication.

—— (2007a) Personal communication.

—— (2007b) Humanities Education Centre on Linking and Development response on DFID consultation on Linking and development, produced for BUILD conference.

—— (2008a) Personal communication.

—— (2008b) HEC DEA Thinkpiece: Thinking about linking.

Cawson, A. (2005) 'Harnessing the international Fiankoma teacher programme for cross-cultural dialogue' *Development Education Journal*, 11.3 ICT in Global Learning Education.

Central Bureau for Educational Visits and Exchanges (1991) *Making the Most of Your Partner School Abroad.* London: CBEVE.

Central Bureau for Educational Visits and Exchanges (1998) *School Partnerships with the South: a handbook for UK schools linking with Africa, Asia, Latin America and the Caribbean.* London: CBEVE.

Commission for Africa (2005) *Our Common Interest: What does the Commission for Africa Say?* DFID, DEA and Commission for Africa.

Cutler, M. (2005) 'Using ICT to explore science locally and share insights globally'. *Development Education Journal*, 11.3 ICT in Global Learning Education.

Davies, L., Harber, C. and Yamashita, H. (2005) *Global Citizenship Education: The needs of teachers and learners.* Birmingham: Centre for International Education and Research, School of Education, University of Birmingham.

Department for Education and Skills (DfES) (2004) Putting the World into World Class Education.

—— (2007) Putting the World into World Class Education Action Plan.

Department for International Development (DFID) (2006) The World Classroom Developing Global Partnerships in Education.

—— (2006) 'DFID Global Schools Partnerships programme announces significant increase in funding'. Press release, 28 June.

—— (2007) DFID Global School Partnerships (DGSP) and Development Education.

Department for International Development/Department for Education and Employment (DFID/DfEE) (2000) *Developing a Global Dimension in the School Curriculum.* London: DfEE.

Department for International Development/Department for Education and Skills (DFID/DfES) (2005) *Developing a Global Dimension in the School Curriculum.* London: DfES.

DFID Global School Partnerships (DGSP) (2006) News Issue 3.

—— (2007) *Partners in Learning: A guide to successful global school partnerships.* (Authors: Ruth Najda and Ali Brownlie Bojang).

DFID Global School Partnerships and IDEAS (2006) 'Good practice network'. Global School Partnerships and Links. Conference Report.

Disney, A. (2003) Building the Professional Knowledge Base of Teacher Educators: Using school linking as a context for developing students' understanding of global citizenship. *Citizenship Education and Teacher Education.*

—— (2004) 'Children's developing images and representations of the school link environment'. In S. Catling and F. Martin (eds), *Researching Primary Geography.* London: Register of Research in Primary Geography.

Doe, B. (2007) Promoting School Partnerships, A report to the Education Committee of the UK UNESCO Commission on the Commonwealth Consortium for Education conference on school linking (Cape Town, December 2006) and some implications of the planned expansion of UK school partnerships for the Commission's work.

Duncan, A. (2005) Communication during debate: the domestic politics of international aid. Global Development Forum 7, London, 16 March.

Dunk, M (2006) 'Home help'. *Developments*, 34.

Edge, K. (2006) Personal communication.

Egan, A. (2006) Personal communication.

—— (2007) Personal communication.

Fricke, H-J. (2006) 'North–South school linking: a review of approaches'. Unpublished report commissioned by Plan International.

—— (2008) Personal communication.

Gaine, C (2006) 'Are twins ever equal?' *One World Linking*, UKOWLA newsletter, 60 Summer.

Garden, B. (2003) 'Getting it right: school exchanges between Norway and the South – evaluating experiences'. *Development Education Journal*, 9.3.

Gerrard, P. (1994) *Turn it Upside Down*. London: Development Education Association.

Global Dimension Trust (2005) Global-ITE Final Report.

—— (2006) Share to Learn Programme (STLP) A new school-linking programme.

Glolinks News (1992) Vol. 1, no. 1.

—— (1993) Vol. 2, no. 2.

Heyes, S. (2006) Personal communication.

Hicks, D. (2005) 'Global education: what does it mean?' In A. Kent and A. Morgan (eds), *The Challenge of the Global Dimension in Education*. London: Institute of Education.

Hillier, F. (2003) 'UK Programmes Case Study: Toot Hill School'. November. Available: <www.lcd.org.uk>

Hillier, J. (2006) 'School linking partnerships and global citizenship'. Research article. citizED project.

Irish Aid (2006) *Irish Aid and Development Education* – Dublin: Department of Foreign Affairs.

—— (2007) Development Education. *Strategy Plan 2007–2011 Promoting public engagement for development*. Dublin: Department of Foreign Affairs.

Jordan, A. (2005) 'One world, one society'. *Development Education Journal*, 11.3 ICT in Global Learning Education.

Knowles, E. (2000) *North–South School Linking and Development Education: An evaluation*. London: Central Bureau.

Komeja, M. (2006) Personal communication.

Leach, R.J. (1969) *International Schools and their Role in the Field of International Education*. Oxford: Pergamon Press.

Learning and Teaching Scotland (2001) *The Global Dimension in the Curriculum*.

—— (2002) 'Education for citizenship: a paper for discussion and development'.

Leftwich, S. (2006a) 'How can the taught curriculum resulting from an international school-to-school link have a measured and substantiated impact upon how students view the world?' Unpublished MA assignment, SWIFT Masters Programme, South West Initiative for Training, Universities of Plymouth and Exeter.

—— (2006b) 'How do the outcomes of CPD arising from the international link at Polesworth High School contribute to personal, departmental and school developments?' Unpublished MA assignment, SWIFT Masters Programme, South West Initiative for Training, Universities of Plymouth and Exeter.

—— (2006c) Personal communication.

Leonard, A. (2004a) 'Geography, global citizenship and school linking'. Unpublished MA dissertation, Institute of Education, University of London.

—— (2004b) 'Impact of school linking on teaching and learning about development issues and global citizenship in secondary geography'. BPRS. Previously accessible: <http://www.teachernet.gov.uk/professionaldevelopment/ resourcesandresearch/bprs/search/index.cfm?report=2167>

—— (2005) 'Lessons from UK secondary schools: school linking and teaching and learning in global citizenship and geography'. *Development Education Journal*, 11.2.

Lissner, J. (1977) *The Politics of Altruism*. Geneva.

LSO National Agency for Global Education (2000) *Soesterberg Declaration on North–South School Linking*. Amsterdam: LSO National Agency for Global Education.

McFarlane, C. (1994) 'Study visits for teachers'. In A. Osler (ed.) *Development Education: Global Perspectives in the Curriculum*. London: Cassell.

Martin, F. (2005) 'North–South school linking as a controversial issue'. *Prospero*, 14.4.

—— (2006) Personal communication.

—— (2007) 'School linking: a controversial issue.' In H. Claire and C. Holden (eds), *The Challenge of Teaching Controversial Issues*. London: Trentham.

Maurice, N. (2003) 'What's this community linking all about?' *Development Education Journal*, 9.2.

Moore, E. (1999) 'Going global'. *Guardian Education*, 21 September.

Najda, R. (2008) Personal communication.

Newell-Jones, K. (2005) *Global-ITE Final Report: Evaluation*. Cheltenham, Glos.: Global Dimension Trust.

Northern Ireland Council for the Curriculum, Examinations and Assessment (CCEA) (2003) *Local and Global Citizenship: A resource for post-primary schools*.

O' Keeffe, C. (2006) *Linking between Ireland and the South. A review and guidelines for good practice*. Dublin: Irish Aid and Suas Education Development.

Oluwole, O. (2003) Personal communication.

OSDE-CSSGJ (2006) 'Open spaces for dialogue and enquiry: methodology'. Nottingham University.

Osler, A. (1994) *Development Education: Global Perspectives in the Curriculum.* London: Cassell.

—— (2004) 'Citizenship and the challenge of global education'. In A. Kent and A. Morgan (eds), *The Challenge of the Global Dimension in Education.* London: Institute of Education.

Oxfam (2006) 'Global Citizenship – what and why'. <www.oxfam.org.uk>

Petersen, T. (2005) 'Community based ICT solutions to school linking: lessons from Young People's Commission for Africa'. *Development Education Journal,* 11.3 ICT in Global Learning Education.

Potts, M. (2004) 'How can I use my own values and my experience of schools in South Africa to influence my own education and the education of others?' Unpublished dissertation, University of Bath.

Qualifications and Curriculum Authority (QCA) (2007) *The Global Dimension in Action. A curriculum planning guide for schools.* London: QCA.

Reibstein, J. (2006) *The Best-kept Secret: Men's and women's stories of lasting love.* London: Bloomsbury.

Scoffham, S. (2007) 'Please Miss, why are they so poor?' *Primary Geographer,* Spring.

—— (2008) Personal communication.

Schirher, S. (2006) Personal communication.

Short, C. (1999) *Education and Our Global Future.* London: DFID.

Stiasny, M. (2005) 'What is internationalism in education?' *Development Education Journal,* 11.3 ICT in Global Learning Education.

Temple, G. (2006a) 'Global citizenship: thinking about linking'. *TES Teacher,* 31 March, p. 14.

—— (2006b) Personal communication.

UK One World Linking Association (UKOWLA) (2006) *One World Linking,* UKOWLA newsletter, 60 Summer.

Watts, M. (2005) 'Celebrating and valuing global citizenship: lessons from a Norwich high school'. *Development Education Journal,* 11.2.

Whitehead, G. (2001) *The Global Footsteps for Schools (GFS) Project. Final report and recommendations.* Cheltenham, Glos.: GlosDEC.

—— (2006) Personal communication.

Williams, P. (2006a) 'Educational enquiry. Oldfield School/Mtengwane School. Evaluating a North/South school link'. Unpublished MA assignment, University of Bath.

—— (2006b) 'Research methods in education unit assignment: evaluating a school link'. Unpublished research proposal, University of Bath.

Wroe, M. and Doney, M. (2005) *The Rough Guide to a Better World and How You Can Make a Difference*. London: Rough Guides.

Websites consulted September 2006 to January 2008: http://www.

8020.ie

bbc.co.uk/worldclass/

britishcouncil.org/globalschools-partnership-advice-agreement.htm

britishcouncil.org/schoolpartnerships-study-visit-funding.htm

britishcouncil.org/globalschools-partners-in-learning.htm

britishcouncil.org/globalschools-resources-orgs

britishcouncil.org/learning-partner-finding.htm

britishcouncil.org/connecting-classrooms

build-online.org.uk

chembakolli.com

citized.info/?strand=1&r_menu=res

citized.info/?strand=4&r_menu=res_art

dea.org.uk/schools/publications.html

deni.gov.uk

developmenteducation.ie/

dea.org.uk/

dfid.gov.uk/news/files/Speeches/wp2006-speeches/beyond-aid230206.asp

dfid.gov.uk/pubs/files/world-classroom

education-action.org

epals.com

globalcentredevon.org.uk

global-development-forum.org

globaldimension.org.uk

globalgateway.org

globalgateway.org.uk/pdf/International-Strategy-support-for-headteachers.pdf

globallinks.org.uk

iearn.org

intedalliance.org

irishaid.gov.ie

lcd.org.uk

ltscotland.org.uk/citizenship/about/index.asp

ltscotland.org.uk/citizenship/globaldimensions/index.asp

neelb.org.uk/teacher/cass/environment-and-society/citizenship

new.wales.gov.uk/docrepos/40382/4038232/4038211/40382910/global-citizenship-e.pdf?lang=en

osdemethodology.org.uk/

oxfam.org.uk

oxfam.org.uk/education/teachersupport/cpd/partnerships/

partnerships.org.uk

plan-uk.org

qca.org.uk/qca_15333.aspx

qca.org.uk/libraryAssets/media/Global_Dimensions

roughguide-betterworld.com

sciaf.org.uk

standards.dfes.gov.uk/schemes2/citizenship/cit17/?view=get

teachernet.gov.uk/professionaldevelopment/tipd/otheropports

throughothereyes.org.uk

towntwinning.org.uk

ukowla.org.uk/main/toolkit.asp

6 Education for global citizenship: towards a clearer agenda for change

Gillian Temple and Anna Luise Laycock[1]

> A vision without action is just a dream; an action without vision just passes time; a vision with an action changes the world.
>
> Nelson Mandela

Introduction

It is often said that education is the most powerful weapon we can use to change the world. But what values and goals lie behind this statement? And what does this mean for the theory and practice of education for global citizenship (E4GC)?

This chapter will introduce some key theoretical and practical issues around the role of E4GC in promoting change in young people and change in the world, and will suggest some directions for the future development of the E4GC movement. In particular, it will consider the following issues:

- Should we be more open about the change we want to see in the world, and the values that drive this change?
- Do we value the role of action sufficiently in this change process?
- How can we better help young people on their journey to become active global citizens?

A chapter of this nature can only introduce the issues, and point towards possible answers. It aims to challenge; and to bring to light the key challenges that face us all in trying to achieve our goals. If it provokes debate and dissent, it has achieved its aim.

Agendas for change

E4GC seeks to achieve positive change in young people and, through young people's attitudes and behaviour, in the world (i.e. individual change and societal change – see Figure 6.1). Oxfam, for example, seeks to develop global citizens who, *inter alia*, are outraged by social injustice, take responsibility for their actions, and are willing to act to make the world a more equitable and sustainable place (Oxfam 1997). Our work forms part of the Development Education (DE) movement's mission to '[develop] the skills, attitudes and values which enable people to work together to bring about change' and '[work] towards achieving a more just and sustainable world in which power and resources are more equitably shared' (DEA 2001: 1).

This change, both at an individual and a societal level, is driven by our values: that which we hold to be right and good. What we see as positive change in young people and the world is based on a conception of what is just (fair) and unjust (unfair) in the world, and what is positive (valued) change in people and society (Laycock 2006). This is our *agenda*: our values-driven vision for change.[2]

A crucial part of the E4GC agenda is the role of young people as agents for change in the world, through the action they take and the

Figure 6.1 Dimensions of change in education for global citizenship

attitudes and values that drive that action. We want young people's behaviour to be driven by their *own* agenda for change, based on a critical understanding of the world. This is the essence of active global citizenship.

E4GC frameworks such as Oxfam's Curriculum for Global Citizenship set out clear outcomes for young people's development, in terms of knowledge, skills and values, in common with mainstream curriculum documents (e.g. national curriculum guidance). However, such frameworks are considerably vaguer about the actions we wish young people to take in the world, and the change we want to see in the world as a consequence of this – that is the societal purpose of education.

This may spring from fear of charges of manipulation, or because we feel a tension between our societal aims and our emphasis on empowering methodologies: respecting the learner and supporting critical thinking, autonomous decision making and self-determined action. However, given that we *do* have certain outcomes we wish to see in young people and the world, it is the authors' belief that we need to articulate fully our aims for change and the values that lie behind these aims: we need a clear agenda.[3]

The benefits of a clear agenda

A clear agenda has two very important benefits for the E4GC (and wider DE) movement:

- It enables us to justify the changes we are working for and the values that drive our work. Mainstream education, just like DE, also has an agenda for social change – the difference is the type of society we are working to create.[4] Making this explicit may give us a hugely powerful argument for mainstreaming an E4GC approach.

- It enables us to open up our goals and values to critical analysis: the questioning, dialogue and dissent that are vital in developing a more inclusive and rigorous approach.[5] This approach is a key tool in developing praxis, a concept central to many DE practitioners' work.

> Before action is taken, the underlying values need to be made explicit. It is then that praxis, the action-reflection-action process, becomes an instrument for initiating and reinforcing the positive macro or micro changes desired or underway.
>
> (Wignaraja 1993: 20)

If we understand the dual (societal and individual) aims of E4GC, as characterised above, making this agenda clear should not compromise our focus on young people. The purposes of E4GC can be cast as intrinsic and instrumental: we value the development of young people as an end in itself, and we also value the contribution young people can make to building a better world. We value change in young people *and* society. And the two aims are essential to each other: if we care about the well-being of young people, we should care about the world in which they live now and in the future; if we care about the world, we should care about the values and actions of young people as citizens now and in the future.

Being explicit about the social change we wish to achieve, therefore, should not diminish our focus on the development of young people. Thus in the simple diagram above (Figure 6.1), we talk of change *in* young people, not *changing* young people. 'Changing' young people implies manipulation – using young people to achieve our ends – whereas 'change in' young people reflects our focus on helping young people to develop themselves, and by extension, society.

So, with our clear agendas, we do steer young people towards certain attitudes and actions, but we do not prescribe them. We hope for certain outcomes from our work, but not to the detriment of our respect for young people's autonomy. In fact, we can only achieve lasting change in young people's attitudes and actions through an educational process which respects young people and enables them to make their own decisions.

Action for change

If we are clear about the changes that we want to see in the world and why, we will be more able to provide a useful framework to help young people take action to bring about that change. This is not just important in terms of achieving societal change through young people; arguably, it is also important for the development of young people themselves.

We value empowerment of young people. But empowerment is not the same as delegation; in fact, giving responsibility without power can be highly disempowering and demotivating. Empowerment involves developing young people's sense of their own power and agency (Holden and Clough 1998b), and one of the best ways of developing this is by helping young people to experience action in support of a better world. True empowerment is not just helping people to understand the issues critically, but also helping them take action to do something about them. Moreover, since action is an important part of the learning process (e.g. Smith 1996; Holden and Clough 1998b), to support young people's global citizenship action is to support young people's global citizenship learning.

Just as we support young people to learn about the issues, should we not, therefore, support them to take action on those issues? At an early stage of skills and understanding, this may take a more structured, directive (but never manipulative) form; as young people develop, we can progress to asking them to design their own actions and manage their own direction (Hart 1992, in Holden and Clough 1998a). To ask the latter of young people with little experience of active global citizenship is a high ask indeed, and could be discouraging to them and their teachers.

The drawbacks of this approach have been well discussed within DE. The notion of young people taking action on global issues without a deep understanding of the complexity of those issues, our complicity in the causes, and the range of possible solutions, may run contrary to DE principles. Indeed, DE asserts its difference from disciplines such as campaigning and fund-raising by virtue of this. Ill-informed actions may not only fail to develop understanding; they might actually reinforce prejudice and misunderstanding. Global citizenship action without global citizenship values is not our goal.

Without disputing any of these concerns, could this be the very reason why E4GC practitioners *need* to engage with young people at the level of ill-informed action? Is it not those who are motivated to take action to change the world, but lack the understanding and attitudes we value, who should be the focus of our attention? Could this be a starting point for the development of global citizenship understanding and attitudes? If so, we need to understand the journey these young people will take towards a higher level of active global citizenship – and how we can support them on that journey.

The active global citizenship journey

Global citizenship is sometimes described as a universal status, or sometimes as comprising different levels or categories of global citizen (e.g. Heater 2002; Dower 2003). We would argue that *active* global citizenship is best seen as a journey: from lower to higher levels of understanding, skills and values, and towards a common destination – a better world.

The metaphor of the journey reflects the conventional concepts of cognitive, emotional and moral development as progressing through levels of competence (Piaget, Kohlberg, etc.), evident in national curricula across the UK and world. It echoes the themes of universality and difference, progression and temporality in global citizenship theory. We are *all* on a global citizenship journey, from our passive status as citizens with moral responsibilities to the rest of the world, to realising a full, active form of global citizenship in which we fulfil those responsibilities to the best of our abilities. Some of us will move further or faster than others – some of us may never take a step forward in recognising and acting on our global responsibilities – and part of that journey is working to build the institutions of the future that will enable us to be fully active global citizens.

Perhaps most importantly, framing global citizenship as a journey allows us to recognise both the validity of young people's development on that journey, and the importance of the destination: the societal change we want to bring about. And it opens up the possibility that across different groups of people there may be different paths to the same destination.[6]

The journey conception of active global citizenship is perhaps more useful than characterising different types of global citizenship as critical or soft, strong or weak, etc.[7] It also has some very important implications for our practice as educators:

- If global citizenship is a journey, we should not expect young people to make that journey instantaneously, or without support.

- Even with our support, just as in conventional education, some young people will not reach the highest levels of critical thinking, skills or values. But they may still want to take action to bring about change in the world.

- If we want to help young people progress on their journey towards fully active global citizenship, we need to *start where they are* and help them to move on.

- We should be careful not to assume that we, as educators, have completed our journeys: we are all developing as global citizens and should continually question our beliefs and practice to ensure that we keep progressing.

Taking action is often the first way young people begin to engage with global issues, at an early stage on their global citizenship journey. We may feel that their desire to take action is not motivated by a sophisticated understanding of the issues and may come from beliefs or motives we do not fully endorse, but the wish to *do something* is significant. It is an expression of caring about the issues, and can be the first step from inertia to movement on a young person's journey.

If we criticise young people's motives rather than encourage their caring, or insist that action can only come *after* fully informed, critical thinking, we risk being a barrier, rather than an enabler, for the young person's development. If we dishearten or deter young people from taking well-meaning action, it is likely that they will simply disengage from us. Thus we lose our opportunity to help those young people move along in their journey, use their experience of taking action as a catalyst for reflection and learning, and develop their understanding and attitudes towards the issues.

If we want to help young people on this journey, we should be wary of polarising 'simplistic' versus 'critical' thinking and motivations for action, and instead focus on how we can utilise this expression of caring to help develop young people's understanding, skills and values. This is a significant theoretical and practical challenge, but is also our biggest opportunity for reaching out to more and more young people.[8]

The same is true of teachers. They also need to move along this journey, both in terms of their understanding, skills and values, and the actions that they can take for change – in their pupils and in the world. So we need to understand the journey that teachers move through as they develop their E4GC practice, and ensure that we are starting where teachers are and helping them progress through the journey, rather than criticising their motives or actions, or failing to develop a positive, ongoing relationship with them.[9]

How we meet this challenge is a question of the utmost importance for E4GC advocates, and for the DE movement in general. It involves examining our agendas for change, reflecting on our values and principles, revisiting how we conceive active global citizenship, and reappraising how we communicate and interact with young people and teachers. We have much thinking and discussion ahead of us, but as a movement we must also maintain a focus on action: if we are committed to helping every young person develop as an active global citizen, and ultimately to changing the world, we need to be ready to change the way we work.

Conclusions

E4GC practitioners have a destination for young people, and for the world, driven by our fundamental values: our agenda. This chapter calls for us to be more open about that agenda, and why we value it. To be explicit about the changes that we want to see in the world, and why, does not mean devaluing our emphasis on change in young people – each is essential to the other.

Being more open about our agenda – our destination – will help us to give young people a framework for action they can take in support of societal change, while also facilitating their own personal develop-ment. Such action has multiple value for E4GC: it helps bring about change in the world; helps develop young people's sense of agency; is an important part of the learning cycle; and is the place where many young people start their global citizenship journey.

Young people need our support to make that journey, and they may start from a place where we would rather they were not, in terms of their attitudes or understanding. But we need to engage with where young people (and teachers) are *now*. This does not mean leaving them there: it means taking them on a journey with us. We need to balance our desire for full understanding and critical thinking with the need to give young people – and teachers – encouragement and the belief that they can make a difference. If we do not, we miss a key opportunity to take E4GC to more and more people – and to help create the change that we want to see in the world.

Notes
1 The views expressed in this chapter are the personal opinions of the authors and do not necessarily reflect those of Oxfam GB.
2 Cf. Reimers' (2006) argument that education policy and practice is driven by a society's conception of 'a good life'. Reimers contends that the broad public purpose of education should not be divorced from the practice of education.
3 Oxfam, for example, might outline its agenda in terms of its overall mission: to work with others to overcome poverty and suffering (i.e. the change it wants to see in the world), and the beliefs and values that guide this. These include the belief that all human lives are of equal value, and that everyone has fundamental

rights, which should be upheld at all times (see <http://www.oxfam.org.uk/about_us/mission.htm> for more details).

4 In the UK, 'the current emphasis in the formal sector is on selecting and preparing individuals for an expanding market economy' (Sterling 1996: 27). Setting out our agenda means proposing an alternative purpose for education, and an alternative type of society.

5 Haydon (2005) notes the importance of cross-cultural dialogue about DE values, for example. The DE community could base this approach on the informal 'discourse ethics' of global ethicists, who seek to create a common core of norms for global citizenship rather than promoting a complete world view (Dower 1999, 2003).

6 This is a huge question for development educators and global citizenship theorists, and one which deserves much more attention than it currently receives. It seems implausible that one model of global citizenship development would be applicable across all genders, cultures, ages, etc.

7 E.g. Sterling 1996; Andreotti 2006.

8 Oxfam's own research shows that it is clear that many young people care about key global issues (90 per cent of young people think it is not fair that poor people across the world do not have the basics in life) and are willing to play their part (89 per cent believe it is everyone's responsibility to try and make the world a better place).

9 Davies et al. (2005) identified a clear lack of confidence amongst teachers when considering global citizenship issues. Teachers felt they lacked skills and knowledge when addressing the issues and feared being seen as 'a failure'. Taking an overly critical, rather than supportive, stance towards these teachers is likely to alienate them rather than encourage them to develop their global citizenship practice.

References

Andreotti, V. (2006) 'Soft versus critical global citizenship education'. *Policy and Practice*, 3 (Autumn), Belfast: Centre for Global Education.

Davies, L., Harber, C. and Yamashita, H. (2005) *Global Citizenship Education: The needs of teachers and learners*. Birmingham: Centre for International Education and Research, School of Education, University of Birmingham.

Development Education Association (2001) *Global Perspectives in Education: The contribution of development education*. London: DEA.

Dower, N. (1999) 'Global ethics and global citizenship'. In N. Dower and J. Williams (eds), (2002) *Global Citizenship: A critical reader*. Edinburgh: Edinburgh University Press.

—— (2003) *An Introduction to Global Citizenship*. Edinburgh: Edinburgh University Press.

Haydon, G. (2005) 'What kind of values education does development education need?' *Development Education Journal*, 11.2, 3–5.

Heater, D. (2002) *World Citizenship: Cosmopolitan thinking and its opponents*. London: Continuum.

Holden, C. and Clough, N. (1998a) (eds), *Children as Citizens: Education for participation*. London: Jessica Kingsley.

Holden, C. and Clough, N. (1998b) '"The child carried on the back does not know the length of the road": the teacher's role in assisting participation'. In C. Holden and N. Clough (eds), *Children as Citizens: Education for participation*. London: Jessica Kingsley.

Laycock, A. (2006) 'Development education, values and social change'. Unpublished paper.

Oxfam Development Education (1997) *A Curriculum for Global Citizenship*. Oxford: Oxfam GB.

Reimers, F. (2006) 'Citizenship, identity and education: examining the public purposes of schools in an age of globalisation'. *Prospects* 36.3, 1–24.

Smith, A. (1996) *Accelerated Learning in the Classroom*. Trowbridge: Redwood Books.

Sterling, S. (1996) 'Education in change'. In J. Huckle and S. Sterling (1996) (eds), *Education for Sustainability*. London: Earthscan.

Wignaraja, P. (1993) 'Rethinking development and democracy'. In P. Wignaraja (ed.), *New Social Movements in the South*. London: Zed Books.

7 Developing a futures dimension in the school curriculum

David Hicks

Introduction

This chapter outlines an important dimension missing from the Department for Education and Skills (DfES) curriculum guidance booklet on the global dimension and that is the futures dimension. The area of 'futures studies' and a potential conceptual framework for a 'futures dimension' are explored and also what needs to be considered in terms of future debate, dialogue and research in this area.

One of the most welcome publications for those working in global and international education is the DfES (2005) curriculum guidance on the need for a global dimension in the school curriculum. This official blessing stands on the shoulders of many educators who have worked for such recognition over the last thirty years. The document provides a platform for the educational initiatives needed to help consolidate awareness and understanding of local–global interdependence (Hicks and Holden 2007).

Figure 7.1 is an important reminder, however, that the curriculum contains both a spatial and temporal dimension. Just as in the 1980s the global dimension was seen to be an often missing element in the curriculum so, since the 1990s, the future has increasingly been seen as missing on the temporal dimension.

Figure 7.1 The spatial and temporal dimensions

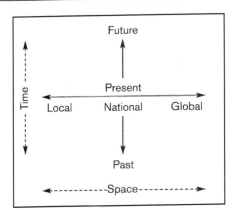

A missing dimension

It is as vital for young people to understand the temporal interrelationships between past, present and future as it is the spatial interrelationships between local, national and global. Yet, if all education is preparation for the future, when, where and how are pupils given the opportunity to explore the futures that they would like to see come about? Whilst historians deal with time past and all teachers deal with time present, explicit exploration of the future is still largely missing from the curriculum.

Gough's (1990) investigation of the portrayal of futures in education revealed three common types of reference: tacit, token and taken for granted. *Tacit futures* are all those which are assumed but remain hidden. Thus whilst the future may not be mentioned in a document assumptions about it are still tacitly present. *Token futures* involve clichés and stereotypes presented in a rhetorical fashion. Gough (1990: 303) notes, 'When one finds "the future" … in the title of an educational document it usually means much less than might be expected.' *Taken-for-granted futures* occur whenever a particular future, or range of futures, is described as if there were no other alternatives. Discussion of the future framed solely in terms of science and technology or a Western world view would be in this category. Gough's research suggests that the future is a missing dimension in education.

The Qualifications and Curriculum Authority (QCA)'s Futures Programme[1] is a case in point since in much of the material (but not all) the future being discussed is tacit, token or taken for granted. Whilst the future of learning, the future of the curriculum and the future of education are very much in the foreground, what is largely missing is any exploration of the future itself. Alternative futures, both local and global, arise out of particular social, cultural and political contexts, as indeed does education. The field of futures studies contains a wealth of expertise on how to explore possible, probable and preferable futures and this has to be a central element in any educational programme that claims to be about futures.

Futures studies

Whilst interest in the future is as old as humanity itself, serious investigation in futures only emerged after the Second World War in the form of strategic planning, technological forecasting, economic analysis and the first major think tanks. Whilst much of this endeavour focused on economic and military forecasting, there were other, largely European, initiatives that were more concerned with how such thinking could be used to help create better social futures (Masini 2006).

Futures studies as a field of academic enquiry emerged in the 1960s and Inayatullah (1993: 236) notes that it 'largely straddles two dominant modes of knowledge – the technical concerned with predicting the future and the humanist concerned with developing a good society'. It is the latter strand which is of particular interest to educators. Key resources in the field are texts such as the *Knowledge Base of Futures Studies* (Slaughter 2005), *Advancing Futures* (Dator 2002), *Foundations of Futures Studies* (Bell 1997) and *The Future is Ours* (May

1996), academic journals such as *Futures* and the *Journal of Futures Studies*, and the World Futures Studies Federation.[2]

Bell (1997) argues that the purpose of futures studies is to 'discover or invent, examine, evaluate and propose possible, probable and preferable futures'. He continues 'futurists seek to know: what can or could be (the possible), what is likely to be (the probable), and what ought to be (the preferable)'. Dator (2005) elaborates further:

> The future cannot be studied because the future does not exist. Futures studies does not ... pretend to study the future. It studies ideas about the future ... (which) often serve as the basis for actions in the present.... Different groups often have very different images of the future. Men's images may differ from women's. Western images may differ from non-Western, and so on....
>
> One of the main tasks of futures studies is to identify and examine the major alternative futures which exist at any given time and place. The future cannot be predicted, but preferred futures can and should be envisioned, invented, implemented, continuously evaluated, revised, and re-envisioned. Thus, another major task of futures studies is to facilitate individuals and groups in formulating, implementing, and re-envisioning their preferred futures.

Elsewhere Dator (2002: 10) argues that despite the variety of people's views of the future, all the images he has encountered, in whatever culture, can be grouped into four broad categories: *continuation* – a 'business as usual' scenario, generally based on notions of continuing economic growth; *collapse* – a 'catastrophe' scenario arising, for example, from economic instability, environmental disaster, terrorist attack; *disciplined society* – based on some set of overarching values, for example traditional, ecological, God-given; *transformational society* – a break from current norms based on 'high-tech' or 'high spirit' values.

Futures studies should not be seen as an internally consistent endeavour. Whilst the key texts referred to above illustrate the breadth of interest, there are also major ideological debates within the field. Most notably this has involved critiques of futures studies as being largely a white Western endeavour (Inayatullah 1998; Sardar 1999; Kapoor 2001) and a largely masculinist discourse (Milojevic 2004).

The futures dimension

Internationally educators use the term 'futures education' or 'futures in education' as shorthand for these concerns. I think that it is more appropriate to talk of the need for a 'futures dimension' in the curriculum and for young people to be able to take a 'futures perspective' on their lives and society more widely. Put at its simplest this describes a form of education which *promotes the knowledge, skills and understanding that are needed in order to think more critically and creatively about the future*. The specific aims of futures education can be formulated as helping teachers and pupils to:

- develop a more *future-oriented* perspective both on their own lives and events in the wider world
- identify and envision *alternative futures* which are just and sustainable
- exercise *critical thinking* skills and the *creative imagination* more effectively
- participate in more thoughtful and informed *decision making* in the present
- engage in active and *responsible citizenship*, both in the local, national and global community, and on behalf of present and future generations.

Unless this temporal element is clearly present in the curriculum, personal, local and global futures will generally remain tacit, token and taken for granted. Thus whilst in relation to a variety of issues we may well help students explore 'Where are we now?' and 'How did we get here?' the crucially empowering questions of 'Where do we want to get to?' and 'How do we get there?' still often remain unexamined.

Key concepts

Underlying the notion of a futures dimension in the curriculum are nine key concepts. These need to underpin all subject areas, as appropriate, and they also help clarify what the futures dimension involves.

1 *State of the world* In the early twenty-first century the state of the world continues to give cause for concern. Issues to do with sustainability, wealth and poverty, peace and conflict, and human rights, all have a major impact both locally and globally. Students need to know about the causes of such problems, how they will affect their lives now and in the future, and the action needed to help resolve them.

2 *Managing change* In periods of rapid social and technological change the past cannot provide an accurate guide to the future. Anticipation and adaptability, foresight and flexibility, innovation and intuition become increasingly essential tools for survival. Students need to develop such skills in order to become more adaptable and proactive towards change.

3 *Views of the future* People's views of the future may vary greatly depending, for example, on age, gender, class and culture, as well as their attitudes to change, the environment and technology. Students need to be aware of how views of the future thus differ and the ways in which this affects people's priorities in the present.

4 *Alternative futures* At any point in time a range of different futures is possible. It is useful to distinguish between probable futures, i.e. those which seem *likely* to come about, and preferable futures, i.e. those one feels *should* come about. Students need to explore a range of probable and preferable futures, from the personal and local to the global.

5 *Hopes and fears* Hopes and fears for the future often influence decision making in the present. Fears can lead to the avoidance of problems rather than their resolution. Clarifying hopes for the

115

future can enhance motivation in the present and thus positive action for change. Students need to explore their own hopes and fears for the future and learn to work creatively with them.

6   *Past/present/future* Interdependence exists across both space and time. Past, present and future are inextricably connected. We are directly linked back in time by the oldest members of the community and forward nearly a century by those born today. Students need to explore these links and to gain a sense of both continuity and change as well as of responsibility for the future.

7   *Visions for the future* The first decade of a new century provides a valuable opportunity for reviewing the state of society. What needs to be left behind and what taken forward? In particular, what visions of a better future are needed to motivate active and responsible citizenship in the present? Students therefore need to develop their skills of envisioning and use of the creative imagination.

8   *Future generations* Economists, philosophers and international lawyers increasingly recognise the rights of future generations. It has been suggested that no generation should inherit less human and natural wealth than the one that preceded it. Students need to discuss the rights of future generations and what the responsibility to uphold these may involve.

9   *Sustainable futures* Current consumerist lifestyles on this planet are increasingly seen as unsustainable, often causing more damage than benefit. A sustainable society would prioritise concern for the environment, the poorest members of the community, and the needs of future generations. Students need to understand how this applies to their everyday lives and possible future employment.

Educational responses

One of the first writers to draw attention to the need for a futures dimension in the school curriculum was Toffler (1974) in his still very relevant *Learning for Tomorrow: The Role of the Future in Education.* His key thesis remains as true now as then: 'All education springs from images of the future and all education creates images of the future. Thus all education, whether so intended or not, is a preparation for the future. Unless we understand the future for which we are preparing, we may do tragic damage to those we teach' (Toffler 1974: cover). It is interesting that he wrote these words in the decade that saw the rise of neoconservative and neo-liberal ideologies which dominate so much of education today (Apple 2006).

Since the 1990s there has been a growing interest in research on young people's images of the future and the implications of this for education (Hicks and Holden 1995; Hicks 2006). Hutchinson (1996) has carried out exciting work in the field of secondary education (including the influences on young people's views of the future), as has Page (2000) in relation to the early childhood curriculum, and Gidley and Inayatullah (2002) in relation to youth futures. A range of case studies of futures in education, from primary to tertiary level, are to be found in Hicks and Slaughter (1998), and a variety of classroom activities can be found in Pike and Selby (1999), Hicks (2001), Slaughter and Bussey (2006). Morgan (2006) and Roberts (2003) have looked at futures in geography whilst Gidley et al. (2004) have explored recent develop-ments in Australia.

A number of interesting studies have explored the nature of young people's probable and preferable futures. Eckersley (1999) reported that Australian youth were particularly concerned about pollution and environmental destruction, the gulf between rich and poor, high unem-ployment, conflict, crime and alienation, discrimination and prejudice, economic difficulties. Eight out of ten 15–24 year olds said that they would prefer a greener, more stable society, with an emphasis on coop-eration, community and family, more equal distribution of wealth and greater economic self-sufficiency. He concluded:

> Young people's preferred futures are undoubtedly idealised and
> utopian. Their significance lies in what they reveal about

fundamental human needs ... and what they expect and what is
being offered to them by world and national leaders.

This echoes much of the research that has been done on envisioning
futures, albeit so far in mainly Western contexts. It also echoes the findings of Elise Boulding (1988) from the numerous envisioning work-
shops that she ran. One should not, however, make the mistake of
thinking that clear images of preferable futures are sufficient in themselves. As Meadows et al. (2005: 272) stress:

> We should say immediately, for the sake of sceptics, that we do not
> believe vision makes anything happen. Vision without action is
> useless. But action without vision is directionless and feeble. Vision is
> absolutely necessary to guide and motivate. More than that, vision
> when widely shared and firmly kept in sight, does bring into being
> new systems.

Conclusions

This chapter has highlighted the value and importance of a futures
dimension within the school curriculum. It has outlined a conceptual
framework for such a dimension and has made reference to existing
studies that refer to this area of study and research. A futures perspective is crucial to effective teaching and learning. By enabling learners
to think more critically and creatively about the forces that create both
probable and preferable futures they are able to engage in more
purposeful and focused action for change. This fulfils what Freire (1994:
9) considers to be one of the tasks of the progressive educator, 'to unveil
opportunities for hope, no matter what the obstacles might be'.

Appendix 7.1: Research needed in futures education

The futures dimension in the curriculum is, as yet, a largely under-researched area (Hicks 2006) and there are a wide number of avenues worthy of exploration. These include:

Images of the future

How do children conceptualise time and the future and how does this vary with age?

- How do children's views of the future vary by gender?
- How do children's views of the future vary by social class?
- How do children's views of the future vary by ethnic group?
- What is the nature of children's probable and preferred futures?
- What emerges from cross-cultural comparisons of the above?

Note: views of the future could be broken down into personal, local, national and global.

Media influences on images

- What images of the future are conveyed by children's books, comics and computer games?
- What images of the future are conveyed by TV advertising?
- What images of the future have been conveyed by popular movies over the last twenty-five years?
- How do such images relate to issues of gender, age, class and Western culture?

Image and action

- How do images of the future affect attitudes and behaviour in the present?
- What determines reactive or proactive stances in relation to the future?
- What changes in attitude and behaviour arise from extended futures-oriented work in a school or classroom?
- What do teaching materials that encourage skills of participation and responsible action look like for different age groups?

Resources and policy

- What do appropriate teaching materials look like for different subject areas and how can subject specialists be encouraged to develop them?
- Which futures methodologies are most useful in the classroom and how can they be related to a range of other learning outcomes?
- How can head teachers, school governors and parents be persuaded of the need for a futures dimension in the curriculum?
- What educational bodies and which key players would need to be influenced in order to gain official backing for such a dimension in the curriculum?

This is not intended to be a complete list but highlights a range of initial research possibilities.

Notes

1 <http://www.qca.org.uk/11232.html>
2 <http://www.wfsf.org>

References

Apple, M. (2006) *Education the 'Right' Way: Markets, standards, god, and inequality,* second edition. London: RoutledgeFalmer.

Bell, W. (1997) *Foundations of Futures Studies,* 2 vols. New Brunswick, NJ: Transaction Publishers.

Boulding, E. (1988) *Building a Global Civic Culture.* New York: Teachers College Press.

Dator, J. (ed.) (2002) *Advancing Futures: Future studies in higher education.* Westport, CT: Praeger.

—— (2005) 'Forward'. In R. Slaughter (ed.), *Knowledge Base of Futures Studies.* CD-ROM. Brisbane: Foresight International <www.foresightinternational.com.au>

Department for Education and Skills (2005) *Developing the Global Dimension in the School Curriculum.* London: DfES.

Eckersley, R. (1999) 'Dreams and experiences: young people's expected and preferred futures and their significance for education'. *Futures,* 31.1, 73–80.

Freire, P. (1994) *A Pedagogy of Hope.* London: Continuum.

Gidley, H. and Inayatullah, S. (eds) (2002) *Youth Futures: Comparative research and transformative visions.* Westport, CT: Praeger.

Gidley, J., Bateman, D. and Smith, C. (2004) *Futures in Education: Principles, practice and potential.* Melbourne: Swinburne University of Technology <www.swin.edu.au/agse/courses/foresight/monographs.htm>

Gough, N. (1990) 'Futures in Australian education: tacit, token and taken for granted'. *Futures,* 22.3, 298–310.

Hicks, D. (2001) *Citizenship for the Future: A practical classroom guide.* Godalming: World Wide Fund for Nature UK.

—— (2006) *Lessons for the Future: The missing dimension in education.* Victoria, BC: Trafford Publishing.

Hicks, D. and Holden, C. (1995) *Visions of the Future: Why we need to teach for tomorrow.* Stoke-on-Trent: Trentham.

Hicks, D. and Holden, C. (eds) (2007) *Teaching the Global Dimension: Key principles and effective practice.* London: RoutledgeFalmer.

Hicks, D. and Slaughter, R. (eds) (1998) *Futures Education: The world yearbook of education 1998.* London: Kogan Page.

Hutchinson, F. (1996) *Educating beyond Violent Futures.* London: Routledge.

Inayatullah, S. (1993) 'From "who am I?" to "when am I?" Framing the shape and time of the future'. *Futures,* 25.3, 235–53.

—— (1998) 'Listening to non-western perspectives'. In D. Hicks and R. Slaughter (eds), *Futures Education: The world yearbook of education 1998*. London: Kogan Page.

Kapoor, R. (2001) 'Future as fantasy: forgetting the flaws'. *Futures*, 33.2, 161–70.

Masini, E. (2006) 'Rethinking futures studies'. *Futures*, 38, 1158–68.

May, G. (1996) *The Future is Ours: Foreseeing, managing and creating the future*. London: Adamantine Press.

Meadows, D., Randers, J. and Meadows, D. (2005) *Limits to Growth: The 30 year update*. London: Earthscan.

Milojevic, I. (2004) *Education Futures: Dominating and contesting visions*. London: RoutledgeFalmer.

Morgan, A. (2006) 'Teaching geography for a sustainable future'. In D. Balderstone (ed.), *Secondary Geography Handbook*. Sheffield: Geographical Association.

Page, J. (2000) *Reframing the Early Childhood Curriculum: Educational imperatives for the future*. London: RoutledgeFalmer.

Pike, G. and Selby, D. (1999) *In the Global Classroom*, 2 vols. Toronto: Pippin Publishing.

Roberts, M. (2003) 'Futures'. In *Learning Through Enquiry: Making sense of geography in the key stage 3 classroom*. Sheffield: Geographical Association.

Sardar, Z. (1999) *Rescuing All our Futures: The future of futures studies*. Westport, CT: Praeger.

Slaughter, R. (ed.) (2005) *Knowledge Base of Futures Studies*. CD-ROM. Brisbane: Foresight International <www.foresightinternational.com.au>

Slaughter, R. with Bussey, M. (2006) *Futures Thinking for Social Foresight*. Taipei: Tamkang University Press. Available: <www.foresightinternational.com.au>

Toffler, A. (1974) *Learning for Tomorrow: The role of the future in education*. New York: Vintage Books.

Index